HEAR A MINUTE

BERYL BYE

THE LUTTERWORTH PRESS
CAMBRIDGE

Day 4

Exodus 20.8-11

'Observe the Sabbath and keep it holy. You have six days in which to do your work, but the seventh day is a day of rest dedicated to me. On that day no one is to work - neither you, your children, your slaves, your animals, nor the foreigners who live in your country. In six days I, the Lord, made the earth, the sky, the sea, and everything in them, but on the seventh day I rested. That is why I, the Lord, blessed the Sabbath and made it holy.'

Thought: Do we make Sunday *different* and a 'rest' day?

Prayer: Dear God, help us to use Sundays for rest and worship, so that our bodies, minds and spirits are refreshed as You intended. Amen.

Day 5

Exodus 20.12

'Respect your father and your mother, so that you may live a long time in the land I am giving you.'

Thought: What does *respect* mean?

Prayer: Heavenly Father, help us to give our parents respect and love and to recognise their needs. Amen.

Day 6

Exodus 20.13-16

'Do not commit murder. Do not commit adultery. Do not steal. Do not accuse anyone falsely.'

Thought: God's laws are never 'out of date'.

Prayer: Dear God, may we keep Your laws in our hearts and minds and please remind us to keep them. Amen.

Day 7

Exodus 20.17

'Do not desire another man's house; do not desire his wife, his slaves, his cattle, his donkeys, or anything else that he owns.'

Thought: Do you think it is wrong to want things that other people have?

Prayer: Dear Father in Heaven, help us to be contented with what we have and not to long for things that we do not have. Amen.

Week 2

For the next three weeks we are going to read parts of a wonderful sermon Jesus preached to a great crowd of people who gathered on a hillside near Galilee to hear His teaching.

Day 1

St Matthew 5.13
'You are like salt for all mankind. But if salt loses its saltiness, there is no way to make it salty again. It has become worthless, so it is thrown out and people trample on it.'

Thought: What happens to stale salt?

Prayer: O God, we know how useful salt is. Make us useful to those with whom we live, work and play. Amen.

Day 2

St Matthew 5.14-16
'You are like light for the whole world. A city built on a hill cannot be hidden. No one lights a lamp and puts it under a bowl; instead he puts it on the lampstand, where it gives light for everyone in the house. In the same way your light must shine before people, so that they will see the good things you do and praise your Father in heaven.'

Thought: What are lights for?

Prayer: Let the light from our lives shine before people so that they will see the good things God does, and praise our Father in heaven. Amen.

Day 3

St Matthew 5.34-7
'But now I tell you: do not use any vow when you make a promise. Do not swear by heaven, for it is God's throne; nor by earth, for it is the resting place for his feet; nor by Jerusalem, for it is the city of the great King. Do not even swear by your head, because you cannot make a single hair white or black. Just say "Yes" or "No" - anything else you say comes from the Evil One.'

Thought: Are the words we speak pleasing to God?

Prayer: O God, teach us to think before we speak, so that all our words may be pleasing to You. Amen.

Day 4

St Matthew 5.38-42

'You have heard that it was said, "An eye for an eye, and a tooth for a tooth." But now I tell you: do not take revenge on someone who wrongs you. If anyone slaps you on the right cheek, let him slap your left cheek too. And if someone takes you to court to sue you for your shirt, let him have your coat as well. And if one of the occupation troops forces you to carry his pack one kilometre, carry it two kilometres. When someone asks you for something, give it to him; when someone wants to borrow something, lend it to him.'

Thought: Do you do more than you are asked to?

Prayer: Loving Lord Jesus, give us the love and grace to forgive those who would quarrel with us and to serve those whom we feel least deserve our help. Amen.

Day 5

St Matthew 5.43-5

'You have heard that it was said, "Love your friends, hate your enemies." But now I tell you: love your enemies and pray for those who persecute you, so that you may become the sons of your Father in heaven. For he makes his sun to shine on bad and good people alike, and gives rain to those who do good and to those who do evil.'

Thought: Think of someone you do not like very much, and pray for them.

Prayer: Dear Father God, I am thinking of . . . Please help me to like them more and help them to want to know You. Amen.

Day 6

St Matthew 5.46-8

'Why should God reward you if you love only the people who love you? Even the tax collectors do that! And if you speak only to your friends, have you done anything out of the ordinary? Even the pagans do that! You must be perfect - just as your Father in heaven is perfect!'

Thought: Make a point of talking to someone you do not like very much.

Prayer: Lord, thank You for our best friends (especially . . .); but help us, over the next few days, to show special kindness to someone outside our close circle. Amen.

Day 7

St Matthew 6.1-4

'Make certain you do not perform your religious duties in public so that people will see what you do. If you do these things publicly, you will not have any reward from your Father in heaven.

'So when you give something to a needy person, do not make a big show of it, as the hypocrites do in the houses of worship and on the streets. They do it so that people will praise them. I assure you, they have already been paid in full. But when you help a needy person, do it in such a way that even your closest friend will not know about it. Then it will be a private matter. And your Father, who sees what you do in private, will reward you.'

Thought: Do a secret good deed.

Prayer: O God, show me a secret good deed that I can do for You, and help me not to tell anyone else about it! Amen.

Week 3

Day 1

St Matthew 6.5-6

'When you pray, do not be like the hypocrites! They love to stand up and pray in the houses of worship and on the street corners, so that everyone will see them. I assure you, they have already been paid in full. But when you pray, go to your room, close the door, and pray to your Father, who is unseen. And your Father, who sees what you do in private, will reward you.'

Thought: How and where should we pray?

Prayer: Lord Jesus, please help us to pray to You, in private, every day. Amen.

Day 2

St Matthew 6.7-13

'When you pray, do not use a lot of meaningless words, as the pagans do, who think that their gods will hear them because their prayers are long. Do not be like them. Your Father already knows what you need before you ask him. This, then, is how you should pray:
    "Our Father in heaven:
    May your holy name be honoured;
    may your Kingdom come;
    may your will be done on earth as it is in heaven.
    Give us today the food we need.
    Forgive us the wrongs we have done,
      as we forgive the wrongs that others have done to us.
    Do not bring us to hard testing,
      but keep us safe from the Evil One."'

Thought: What is the meaning of the saying: 'Familiarity breeds contempt'?

Prayer: Pray the Lord's prayer, in the version most familiar to you.

Day 3

St Matthew 6.14-15

'If you forgive others the wrongs they have done to you, your Father in heaven will also forgive you. But if you do not forgive others, then your Father will not forgive the wrongs you have done.'

Thought: Is there anything for which you have not 'forgiven others'?

Prayer: O Lord Jesus, help us to forgive others (especially . . .) as You have forgiven us. Amen.

Day 4

St Matthew 6.19-21

'Do not store up riches for yourself here on earth, where moths and rust destroy, and robbers break in and steal. Instead, store up riches for yourselves in heaven, where moths and rust cannot destroy, and robbers cannot break in and steal. For your heart will always be where your riches are.'

Thought: What kind of riches can we 'store up in heaven'?

Prayer: Lord Jesus, please help us to be rich in kind words and good deeds, doing everything because of our love for You. Amen.

Day 5

St Matthew 6.24-6

'No one can be a slave of two masters; he will hate one and love the other; he will be loyal to one and despise the other. You cannot serve both God and money.

'This is why I tell you not to be worried about the food and drink you need in order to stay alive, or about clothes for your body. After all, isn't life worth more than food? And isn't the body worth more than clothes? Look at the birds flying around: they do not sow seeds, gather a harvest and put it in barns; yet your Father in heaven takes care of them! Aren't you worth much more than birds?'

Thought: Who is *our* Master?

Prayer: Our Lord and Master, give us a simple trust in You, and help us not to worry about our daily needs, for if we are faithful servants, we know You will provide for us. Amen.

Day 6

St Matthew 6.27-30

'Can any of you live a bit longer by worrying about it?

'And why worry about clothes? Look how the wild flowers grow: They do not work or make clothes for themselves. But I tell you that not even King Solomon with all his wealth had clothes as beautiful as one of these flowers. It is God who clothes the wild grass - grass that is here today and gone tomorrow, burnt up in the oven. Won't he be all the more sure to clothe you? How little faith you have!'

Thought: Is *needing* clothes, different from *wanting* them?

Prayer: O God our Father, thank You for clothes for all occasions. Give us an active concern for those who have no clothes or shoes and lack the money to buy them. Amen.

Day 7

St Matthew 6.31-4

'So do not start worrying: "Where will my food come from? or my drink? or my clothes? (These are the things the pagans are always concerned about.) Your Father in heaven knows that you need all these things. Instead, be concerned above everything else with the Kingdom of God and with what he requires of you, and he will provide you with all these other things. So do not worry about tomorrow; it will have enough worries of its own. There is no need to add to the troubles each day brings.'

Thought: Do not worry about tomorrow until you have sorted out today.

Prayer: Father, thank You for all the blessings You have given us today (especially . . .). Please take away worries about tomorrow, because we know You can deal with them when the time comes. Amen.

Week 4

At the end of this week we will read some verses from The Psalms, which is a collection of poems, songs, and prayers written by different people through the ages, and used by the Jewish people in their worship.

Day 1

St Matthew 7.1-5

'Do not judge others, so that God will not judge you, for God will judge you in the same way as you judge others, and he will apply to you the same rules you apply to others. Why, then, do you look at the speck in your brother's eye, and pay no attention to the log in your own eye? How dare you say to your brother, "Please, let me take that speck out of your eye", when you have a log in your own eye? You hypocrite! First take the log out of your own eye, and then you will be able to see clearly to take the speck out of your brother's eye.'

Thought: Are we more concerned with other people's faults than our own?

Prayer: Lord Jesus, help us to see our own faults more clearly than the faults of others. Amen.

Day 2

St Matthew 7.7-11

'Ask, and you will receive; seek, and you will find; knock, and the door will be opened to you. For everyone who asks will receive, and anyone who seeks will find, and the door will be opened to him who knocks. Would any of you who are fathers give your son a stone when he asks for bread? Or would you give him a snake when he asks for a fish? Bad as you are, you know how to give good things to your children. How much more, then, will your Father in heaven give good things to those who ask him?'

Thought: When we ask, do we expect to receive?

Prayer: O God our Father, may we have the faith to expect answers to our prayers. Amen.

Day 3

St Matthew 7.12-14

'Do for others what you want them to do for you: this is the meaning of the Law of Moses and of the teachings of the prophets.

Go in through the narrow gate, because the gate to hell is wide and the road that leads to it is easy, and there are many who travel it. But the gate to life is narrow and the way that leads to it is hard, and there are few people who find it.'

Thought: Wide and easy, or narrow and hard! Which *gate* have you chosen - and why?

Prayer: Loving Saviour, lead us through the narrow gate and along the hard way, because we know this is the only way to heaven. Amen.

Day 4

St Matthew 7.15-17
'Be on your guard against false prophets; they come to you looking like sheep on the outside, but on the inside they are really like wild wolves. You will know them by what they do. Thorn bushes do not bear grapes, and briars do not bear figs. A healthy tree bears good fruit, but a poor tree bears bad fruit.'

Thought: What kind of 'tree' are you?

Prayer: We know, O Lord, that people judge us by the way we behave. Help us to bring forth the good fruit that brings glory to Your Name. Amen.

Day 5

St Matthew 7.21
'Not everyone who calls me "Lord, Lord" will enter the Kingdom of heaven, but only those who do what my Father in heaven wants them to do.'

Thought: What does the saying, 'Actions speak louder than words,' mean?

Prayer: Lord, forgive us when the way we talk and think or behave does not match the name of 'Christian' that we bear. Amen.

Day 6

Psalm 34.11-14
Come my young friends, and listen to me,
    and I will teach you to honour the Lord.
Would you like to enjoy life?
Do you want long life and happiness?
Then hold back from speaking evil and from telling lies.
Turn away from evil and do good; strive for peace with all your heart.

Thought: What is the secret of happiness?

Prayer: Please God, help us to turn away from evil and do good, and to strive for peace with all our heart. Amen.

Day 7

Psalm 37.3-4

> Trust in the Lord and do good; live in the land and be safe.
> Seek your happiness in the Lord, and he will give you your
> heart's desire.

Thought: What *is* your 'heart's desire' at this time?

Prayer: Lord, help us to seek our happiness in the things that please You, because then we know that You will give us our heart's desire. Amen.

Week 5

We are going to begin the adventures of a boy called Joseph, who was his father's favourite son but was hated by his older brothers.

Day 1

Genesis 37.1-2

Jacob continued to live in the land of Canaan, where his father had lived, and this is the story of Jacob's family.

Joseph, a young man of seventeen, took care of the sheep and goats with his brothers, the sons of Bilhah and Zilpah, his fathers's concubines. He brought bad reports to his father about what his brothers were doing.

Thought: Are you guilty of 'tale-telling' - or giving 'bad reports'?

Prayer: Lord Jesus, we confess how quick we are to complain of other people's behaviour. Forgive us, and help us to keep silent when it is wise to do so. Amen.

Day 2

Genesis 37.3-4

Jacob loved Joseph more than all his other sons, because he had been born to him when he was old. He made a long robe with full sleeves for him. When his brothers saw that their father loved Joseph more than he loved them, they hated their brother so much that they would not speak to him in a friendly manner.

Thought: It is dangerous to have favourites!

Prayer: Dear Father God, help us not to stir up jealousy and hatred by treating some people more generously than others. Amen.

Day 3

Genesis 37.5-7

One night Joseph had a dream, and when he told his brothers about it, they hated him even more. He said, 'Listen to the dream I had. We were all in the field tying up sheaves of wheat, when my sheaf got up and stood up straight. Yours formed a circle round mine and bowed down to it.'

Thought: There is a time to speak and a time to be silent!

Prayer: Heavenly Father, we realise how much of our conversation is unprofitable. Help us to choose our words with tact and love. Amen.

Day 4

Genesis 37.8-10

'Do you think you are going to be a king and rule over us?' his brothers asked. So they hated him even more because of his dreams and because of what he said about them.

Then Joseph had another dream and said to his brothers, 'I had another dream, in which I saw the sun, the moon, and eleven stars bowing down to me.'

He also told the dream to his father, and his father scolded him: 'What kind of a dream is that? Do you think that your mother, your brothers, and I are going to come and bow down to you?'

Thought: We do not always learn from our mistakes!

Prayer: Dear God, often we fail to learn from our mistakes and so repeat them. Give us strength to conquer our 'regular' sins. Amen.

Day 5

Genesis 37.11-14

Joseph's brothers were jealous of him, but his father kept thinking about the whole matter.

One day when Joseph's brothers had gone to Shechem to take care of their father's flock, Jacob said to Joseph, 'I want you to go to Shechem, where your brothers are taking care of the flock.'

Joseph answered, 'I am ready.'

His father said, 'Go and see if your brothers are safe and if the flock is all right; then come back and tell me.' So his father sent him on his way from the Valley of Hebron.

Thought: Do we do what we are told by God, our parents, or those who are in positions of authority over us?

Prayer: Lord, teach us to be obedient to You, to our parents, and to those who have authority over us.

Day 6

Genesis 37.18-20

They saw him in the distance, and before he reached them, they plotted against him and decided to kill him. They said to one another, 'Here comes that dreamer. Come on now, let's kill him and throw his body into one of the dry wells. We can say that a wild animal killed him. Then we will see what becomes of his dreams.'

Thought: Planned and deliberate cruelty is surely the hardest to forgive.

Prayer: Lord Jesus, we confess that we are sometimes deliberately unkind to other people. Please forgive us and help us to show them Your love. Amen.

Day 7

Genesis 37.21-2

Reuben heard them and tried to save Joseph. 'Let's not kill him,' he said. 'Just throw him into this well in the wilderness, but don't hurt him.' He said this, planning to save him from them and send him back to his father.

Thought: It takes courage to stand out against a crowd.

Prayer: Father God, give us the courage to stand out against the crowd, even when it is hard to do so. Amen.

Week 6

Day 1

Genesis 37.23-5

When Joseph came up to his brothers, they ripped off his long robe with full sleeves. Then they took him and threw him into the well, which was dry.

While they were eating, they suddenly saw a group of Ishmaelites travelling from Gilead to Egypt. Their camels were loaded with spices and resins.

Thought: It is not the clothes that matter - it is the person underneath!

Prayer: Lord, we confess that we often pay a lot of attention to the clothes we wear; help us to recognise that you are interested in what we are, and not how we look. Amen.

Day 2

Genesis 37.26-8

Judah said to his brothers, 'What will we gain by killing our brother and covering up the murder? Let's sell him to these Ishmaelites. Then we won't have to hurt him; after all, he is our brother, our own flesh and blood.' His brothers agreed, and when some Midianite traders came by, the brothers pulled Joseph out of the well and sold him for twenty pieces of silver to the Ishmaelites, who took him to Egypt.

Thought: We should never seek gain from other people's misfortunes.

Prayer: Father, help us to remember that all men are our brothers, and save us from seeking to profit by exploiting the misfortunes of others, and turning them to our own advantage. Amen.

Day 3

Genesis 37.29-31

When Reuben came back to the well and found that Joseph was not there, he tore his clothes in sorrow. He returned to his brothers and said, 'The boy is not there! What am I going to do?'
Then they killed a goat and dipped Joseph's robe in its blood. They took the robe to their father and said, 'We found this. Does it belong to your son?'

Thought: It is easy to make a bad situation worse.

Prayer: Lord, forgive us when we lie and deceive in an attempt to cover up wrong actions. Remind us that You know everything and are prepared to forgive everything if we are truly sorry. Amen.

Day 4

Genesis 37.33-4

He recognised it and said, 'Yes, it is his! Some wild animal has killed him. My son Joseph has been torn to pieces!'

Jacob tore his clothes in sorrow and put on sackcloth. He mourned for his son a long time.

Thought: Do not jump to conclusions!

Prayer: Lord, so often we are ready to believe the worst. Make us wary of over-hasty judgements. Amen.

Day 5

Genesis 37.35-6

All his sons and daughters came to comfort him, but he refused to be comforted and said, 'I will go down to the world of the dead still mourning for my son.' So he continued to mourn for his son Joseph.

Meanwhile, in Egypt, the Midianites had sold Joseph to Potiphar, one of the king's officers, who was the captain of the palace guard.

Thought: To each his sufferings; all are men,
    Condemned alike to groan;
    The tender for another's pain,
    Th' unfeeling for his own.
                          Thomas Gray (1716-71)

Prayer: Almighty God, remind us that nights of sorrow can be followed by unexpected days of joy, and save us from the sin of continuing self-pity. Amen.

Day 6

Genesis 39.1-3

Now the Ismaelites had taken Joseph to Egypt and sold him to Potiphar, one of the king's officers, who was the captain of the palace guard. The Lord was with Joseph and made him successful. He lived in the house of his Egyptian master, who saw that the Lord was with Joseph and had made him successful in everything he did.

Thought: God needs successful servants as well as successful masters in his employ!

Prayer: Lord, help us to see 'success' in terms of pleasing You in the particular place that You have put us. Amen.

Day 7

Genesis 39.4-5

Potiphar was pleased with him and made him his personal servant; so he put him in charge of his house and everything he owned. From then on, because of Joseph the Lord blessed the household of the Egyptian and everything that he had in his house and in his fields.

Thought: Do you bring blessing to your home, your school, your workplace, your family, or your church?

Prayer: Help us to be a blessing, Lord, to our family, our friend, and to those with whom we work. For Your sake. Amen.

Joseph went on to become Prime Minister of Egypt -
but that is another story!

Week 7

*This week's readings are parts of letters written by Paul and John,
to help Christians lead the kind of lives that please God.*

Day 1

Galatians 6.1-2

My brothers, if someone is caught in any kind of wrongdoing, those of you
who are spiritual should set him right; but you must do it in a gentle way.
And keep an eye on yourselves, so that you will not be tempted, too. Help
to carry one another's burdens, and in this way you will obey the law of
Christ.

Thought: Do we criticise, or help?

Prayer: Lord, help us to carry one another's burdens, so that, in this way,
we obey the law of Christ. Amen.

Day 2

Galatians 6.7-8

Do not deceive yourselves; no one makes a fool of God. A person will reap
exactly what he sows. If he sows in the field of his natural desires, from
it he will gather the harvest of death; if he sows in the field of the Spirit,
from the Spirit he will gather the harvest of eternal life.

Thought: We will only reap what we have sown.

Prayer: God our Father, help us to sow in this life the seeds of good works
so that our harvest may be a plentiful one. Amen.

Day 3

Galatians 6.9-10

So let us not become tired of doing good; for if we do not give up, the time
will come when we will reap the harvest. So then, as often as we have the
chance, we should do good to everyone, and especially to those who
belong to our family in the faith.

Thought: Is there someone in your Church 'family' who needs help today?

Prayer: Lord, remind us, as we wait quietly before You, of anyone who
may specially need our love and care today. Amen.

Day 4

1 John 2.3-6

If we obey God's commands, then we are sure that we know him. If someone says that he knows him, but does not obey his commands, such a person is a liar and there is no truth in him. But whoever obeys his word is the one whose love for God has really been made perfect. This is how we can be sure that we are in union with God: whoever says that he remains in union with God should live just as Jesus Christ did.

Thought: Are we living as Jesus did?

Prayer: Lord Jesus, help us to live as You lived, loving and obeying God our Father and serving our fellow men. Amen.

Day 5

1 John 2.15-17

Do not love the world or anything that belongs to the world. If you love the world, you do not love the Father. Everything that belongs to the world - what the sinful self desires, what people see and want, and everything in this world that people are so proud of - none of this comes from the Father; it all comes from the world. The world and everything in it that people desire is passing away; but he who does the will of God lives for ever.

Thought: There is nothing wrong with the world - it is the people in it! Do you agree?

Prayer: Lord Jesus, we know that we have to choose between the passing pleasures of this world and the lasting joys of the next. Help us to choose wisely. Amen.

Day 6

1 John 3.16-18

This is how we know what love is: Christ gave his life for us. We too, then, ought to give our lives for our brothers! If a rich person sees his brother in need, yet closes his heart against his brother, how can he claim that he loves God? My children, our love should not be just words and talk; it must be true love, which shows itself in action.

Thought: Do you see yourself as *rich*?

Prayer: Father, we have so much to be thankful for; help us to have open hands, open hearts and open purses to supply our brothers who are in need. Amen.

Day 7

1 John 4.7-11

Dear friends, let us love one another, because love comes from God. Whoever loves is a child of God and knows God. Whoever does not love does not know God, for God is love. And God showed his love for us by sending his only Son into the world, so that we might have life through him. This is what love is; it is not that we have loved God, but that he loved us and sent his Son to be the means by which our sins are forgiven. Dear friends, if this is how God loved us, then we should love one another.

Thought: Loving is often demonstrated by giving.

Prayer: Dear Heavenly Father, You showed Your love for us by giving Your Son to die for our sins; may we show our love for others by sacrificing ourselves for them. Amen.

Week 8

During the next three weeks we are going to read about the adventures of Ruth - a young woman, who, after the death of her husband, went with her mother-in-law to live in Bethlehem, where she eventually found a new husband.

Day 1

Ruth 1.1-5

Long ago, in the days before Israel had a king, there was a famine in the land. So a man named Elimelech, who belonged to the clan of Ephrath and who lived in Bethlehem in Judaea, went with his wife Naomi and their two sons Mahlon and Chilion to live for a while in the country of Moab. While they were living there, Elimelech died, and Naomi was left alone with her two sons, who married Moabite girls, Orpah and Ruth. About ten years later Mahlon and Chilion also died, and Naomi was left all alone, without husband or sons.

Thought: In times of great sorrow Jesus can be our comfort.

Prayer: Dear Father God, we ask You to comfort all those who have lost someone they love (especially . . .). Give them Your courage, Your comfort, and Your strength, we pray You. Amen.

Day 2

Ruth 1.6-9

Some time later Naomi heard that the Lord had blessed his people by giving them a good harvest; so she got ready to leave Moab with her daughters-in-law. They started out together to go back to Judah, but on the way she said to them, 'Go back home and stay with your mothers. May the Lord be as good to you as you have been to me and to those who have died. And may the Lord make it possible for each of you to marry again and have a home.'

Thought: What seems like an end can prove to be a new beginning.

Prayer: Father God, help us, like Naomi, to look forward and not back, when life brings great changes. Amen.

Day 3

Ruth 1.9-14

So Naomi kissed them good-bye. But they started crying and said to her, 'No! We will go back with you to your people.'

'You must go back, my daughters,' Naomi answered. 'Why do you want to come with me? Do you think I could have sons again for you to marry? Go back home for I am too old to get married again. Even if I thought there was still hope, and so got married tonight and had sons, would you wait until they had grown up? Would this keep you from marrying someone else? No, my daughters, you know that's impossible. The Lord has turned against me, and I feel very sorry for you.'

Again they started crying. Then Orpah kissed her mother-in-law and went back home, but Ruth held on to her.

Thought: Unselfish love wants the best for others.

Prayer: Please God give us the kind of love that cares more about others than ourselves. Amen.

Day 4

Ruth 1.15-18

So Naomi said to her, 'Ruth, your sister-in-law, has gone back to her people and to her god. Go back home with her.'

But Ruth answered, 'Don't ask me to leave you! Let me go with you. Wherever you go, I will go; wherever you live, I will live. Your people will be my people, and your God will be my God. Wherever you die, I will die, and that is where I will be buried. May the Lord's worst punishment come upon me if I let anything but death separate me from you.'

When Naomi saw that Ruth was determined to go with her she said nothing more.

Thought: Nothing can change the mind of someone who is really determined.

Prayer: Father God, when we feel it is right to go in a certain direction, give us the determination to follow Your leading. Amen.

Day 5

Ruth 1.19-21

They went on until they came to Bethlehem. When they arrived, the whole town got excited, and the women there exclaimed, 'Is this really Naomi?'

'Don't call me Naomi,' she answered; 'call me Marah, because

Almighty God has made my life bitter. When I left here, I had plenty, but the Lord has brought me back without a thing.'

Thought: Are we always ready to blame God for our troubles?

Prayer: Dear God, when things go wrong and we blame You, forgive us and strengthen our faith to believe in Your continuing love and care. Amen.

Day 6

Ruth 2.1-3

Naomi had a relative named Boaz, a rich and influential man who belonged to the family of her husband Elimelech. One day Ruth said to Naomi, 'Let me go to the fields to gather the corn that the harvest workers leave. I am sure to find someone who will let me work with him.' Naomi answered 'Go ahead my daughter.'

So Ruth went out to the fields and walked behind the workers, picking up the corn.

Thought: Ruth was a 'worker' not 'a drone'!

Prayer: Lord, help each one of us to work willingly at school, at home, and in our jobs. We also pray for those who are unable to find a job today (especially . . .). Give them the energy and the motivation to go out and seek employment even though they may feel depressed and discouraged. Amen.

Day 7

Ruth 2.3, 8-9

It so happened that she was in a field that belonged to Boaz . . .

Then Boaz said to Ruth, 'Let me give you some advice. Don't pick up corn anywhere except in this field. Work with the women here, watch them to see where they are reaping and stay with them. I have ordered my men not to molest you. And whenever you are thirsty, go and drink from the water jars that they have filled.'

Thought: The more we have - the more we should give away.

Prayer: Lord Jesus, make us mindful of the needs of others and quick to help them. Amen.

Week 9

Day 1

Ruth 2.10-13

Ruth bowed down with her face touching the ground, and said to Boaz, 'Why should you be so concerned about me? Why should you be so kind to a foreigner?'

Boaz answered, 'I have heard about everything that you have done for your mother-in-law since your husband died. I know how you left your own father and mother and your own country and how you came to live among a people you had never known before. May the Lord reward you for what you have done. May you have a full reward from the Lord God of Israel, to whom you have come for protection!'

Ruth answered, 'You are very kind to me, sir. You have made me feel better by speaking gently to me . . . '

Thought: Do we ever make people feel better by speaking gently to them?

Prayer: Dear Father God, help us to be as gentle and understanding in our dealings with other people, as You are with us. Amen.

Day 2

Ruth 2.14-17

At meal-time Boaz said to Ruth, 'Come and have a piece of bread and dip it in the sauce.' So she sat with the workers, and Boaz passed some roasted grain to her. She ate until she was satisfied, and she still had some food left over. After she had left to go on picking up corn, Boaz ordered the workers, 'Let her pick it up even where the bundles are lying and don't say anything to stop her. Besides that, pull out some corn from the bundles and leave it for her to pick up.'

So Ruth went on gathering corn in the field until evening, and when she had beaten it out, she found she had nearly ten kilogrammes.'

Thought: It takes imagination to offer help that can be accepted without embarrassment.

Prayer: Lord, show us how to be thoughtful and tactful about the way we give so that people can accept help without embarrassment. Amen.

Day 3

Ruth 2.19-21

So Ruth told Naomi that she had been working in a field belonging to a man named Boaz.

'May the Lord bless Boaz!' Naomi exclaimed, 'The Lord always keeps his promises to the living and the dead.' And she went on, 'That man is a close relative of ours, one of those responsible for taking care of us.'

Then Ruth said, 'Best of all, he told me to keep picking up corn with his workers until they finish the harvest.'

Thought: Do we 'feel responsible' for taking care of our relatives?

Prayer: Please help us to have true concern for our relatives, Lord, especially those who have no one else to care for them. Amen.

Day 4

Ruth 3.1, 2, 4, 6

Some time later Naomi said to Ruth, 'I must find a husband for you, so that you will have a home of your own. Remember that this man Boaz, whose women you have been working with, is our relative . . . Be sure to notice where he lies down, and after he falls asleep, go and lift the covers and lie down at his feet. He will tell you what to do . . .'

So Ruth went to the threshing place and did just what her mother-in-law had told her.

Thought: We do not always understand foreign customs!

Prayer: Almighty God, we confess we often find the customs of people of other countries very strange. Remind us that we are all Your children and that You understand us and deal with us all as individuals. Amen.

Day 5

Ruth 3.8, 9, 10, 12, 13

During the night he [Boaz] woke up suddenly, turned over, and was surprised to find a woman lying at his feet. 'Who are you?' he asked.

'It's Ruth, sir,' she answered. 'Because you are a close relative, you are responsible for taking care of me. So please marry me.'

'The Lord bless you,' he said . . . 'It is true that I am a close relative and am responsible for you, but there is a man who is a closer relative than I am. Stay here the rest of the night, and in the morning we will find out whether or not he will take responsibility for you. If so, well and good; if not then I swear by the living Lord that I will take the responsibility.'

Thought: Straight talking can prove the best way to solve difficulties!

Prayer: Lord, please guide us in all our dealings and show us when to speak out and when to be silent. Amen.

Day 6

Ruth 3.14-15

So she lay there at his feet, but she got up before it was light enough for her to be seen, because Boaz did not want anyone to know that she had been there.

Boaz said to her, 'Take off your cloak and spread it out here.'

She did, and he poured out nearly twenty kilogrammes of barley and helped her to lift it on her shoulder. Then she returned to the town with it.

Thought: Do we protect other people's reputations?

Prayer: Lord, we know how easy it is to cause harm to a person by misjudging their actions. Please help us, like Boaz, to be careful to protect, not damage, the reputations of other people. Amen.

Day 7

Ruth 3.16-18

When she arrived home her mother-in-law asked her, 'How did you get on, my daughter?'

Ruth told her everything that Boaz had done for her. She added, 'He told me I must not come back to you empty-handed, so he gave me all this barley.'

Naomi said to her, 'Now be patient, Ruth, until you see how this all turns out. Boaz will not rest today until he settles the matter.'

Thought: 'Be patient . . . until you see how this turns out . . . '

Prayer: Help us, Lord, not to be hasty in making decisions, but to try to be patient when we need to wait and see how things will 'turn out.' Amen.

Week 10

Day 1

Ruth 4.1-2

Boaz went to the meeting place at the town gate and sat down there. Then Elimelech's nearest relative, the man who Boaz had mentioned, came by, and Boaz called to him, 'Come over here, my friend, and sit down.' So he went over and sat down. Then Boaz got ten of the leaders of the town and asked them to sit down there too.

Thought: It is good when family problems can be sorted out at a friendly meeting.

Prayer: Lord, when we have family problems, help us to follow the example of Boaz, calling together those concerned so that things may be sorted out in a friendly way. Amen.

Day 2

Ruth 4.2-4

When they were seated he said to his relative. 'Now that Naomi has come back from Moab, she wants to sell the field that belonged to our relative Elimelech, and I think you ought to know about it. Now then, if you want it, buy it in the presence of these men sitting here. But if you don't want it, say so, because the right to buy it belongs first to you and then to me.'
The man said 'I will buy it.'

Thought: STRAIGHT FORWARD DEALING! - the golden rule for Christians buying or selling land or property!

Prayer: Father God, we know that the buying and selling of property or land can often result in a great deal of ill-feeling; help us to behave in an honest and straightforward manner when we are concerned. Amen.

Day 3

Ruth 4.5-6

Boaz said, 'Very well, but if you buy the field from Naomi, then you are also buying Ruth, the Moabite widow, so that the field will stay in the dead man's family.'
The man answered, 'In that case I will give up my right to buy the field, because it would mean that my own children would not inherit it. You buy it; I would rather not.'

Thought: Do you ever break promises or back out of agreements?

Prayer: Lord Jesus, we sometimes make promises but fail to keep them. Help us, as Christians, to keep our word, and not let people down. Amen.

Day 4

Ruth 4.9-10
Then Boaz said to the leaders and all the others there, 'You are all witnesses today that I have bought from Naomi everything that belonged to Elimelech and to his sons Chilion and Mahlon. In addition, Ruth the Moabite, Mahlon's widow, becomes my wife. This will keep the property in the dead man's family, and his family line will continue among his people and in his town. You are witnesses to this today.'

Thought: Increased wealth brings increased responsibility.

Prayer: Heavenly Father, remind us that increased wealth and prosperity brings with it increased responsibility, and help us to remember that of the one who has much, much will be expected. Amen.

Day 5

Ruth 4.11-12
The leaders and the others said, 'Yes, we are witnesses. May the Lord make your wife become like Rachel and Leah, who bore many children to Jacob. May you become rich in the clan of Ephrath and famous in Bethlehem. May the children that the Lord will give you by this young woman make your family like the family of Perez, the son of Judah and Tamar.'

Thought: There is no guarantee that doing the right thing will result in material prosperity!

Prayer: Lord, help us to do the right thing because we love You and want to please You, and not for any hope of gain. Amen.

Day 6

Ruth 4.13-14
So Boaz took Ruth home as his wife. The Lord blessed her, and she became pregnant and had a son. The women said to Naomi, 'Praise the Lord! He has given you a grandson today to take care of you. May the boy become famous in Israel!'

Thought: Grandchildren are a great joy.

Prayer: Almighty God, thank You for grandmothers and grandfathers, and for the special relationships that develop between children and their grandparents. Please bless our grandparents/grandchildren today, and help us to find ways to show them how much we love them. Amen.

Day 7

Ruth 5.15-17

'Your daughter-in-law loves you, and has done more for you than seven sons. And now she has given you a grandson who will bring new life to you and give you security in your old age.' Naomi took the child, held him close, and took care of him.

Thought: Young children gain security from being 'held close'.

Prayer: Dear Father in Heaven, thank You for giving us the ability to 'hold close' those we love; and, as we do so, may our love for them overflow into silent prayer for their well-being. Amen.

[Happy ending.]
Obed (Ruth's son) became the father of Jesse, who was the father of King David, who was an ancestor of the Lord Jesus - so we can see how Naomi and Ruth's former sorrows became part of a 'pattern' in God's amazing plan to bring salvation to the world.

Week 11

*The Old Testament book of Proverbs is a collection of moral and
religious teaching in the form of sayings and proverbs. They are
about family relationships, business dealings, etiquette, self-control,
humility, patience, respect for the poor and loyalty to friends,
so they have a lot to say to us today.*

Day 1

Proverbs 1.1-3
The proverbs of Solomon, son of David and king of Israel.

Here are proverbs that will help you to recognise wisdom and good
advice, and understand sayings with deep meaning. They can teach you
how to live intelligently and how to be honest, just and fair.

Thought: Are you willing to take good advice?

Prayer: Lord, please help us to be honest, just and fair, and to give (and
take) good advice. Amen.

Day 2

Proverbs 1.4-6
They can make an inexperienced person clever and teach young men
how to be resourceful. These problems can even add to the knowledge of
wise men and give guidance to the educated, so that they can understand
the hidden meanings of proverbs and the problems that wise men raise.

Thought: We should never think we are too clever to learn!

Prayer: God of all power and might, teach and guide us as we try to
understand the many difficult problems of today's world, and help us to
learn from others and from our own experiences. Amen.

Day 3

Proverbs 1.7-10
To have knowledge you must first have reverence for the Lord. Stupid
people have no respect for wisdom and refuse to learn.

Pay attention to what your father and mother tell you, my son. Their
teaching will improve your character as a handsome turban or necklace
improves your appearance.

When sinners tempt you, my son, don't give in.

Thought: 'When sinners tempt you - don't give in!'

Prayer: Lord Jesus, help us not to give in when we are tempted to do wrong, and make us the kind of people who are willing to learn. Amen.

Day 4

Proverbs 3.1-4

Don't forget what I teach you, my son. Always remember what I tell you to do. My teaching will give you a long and prosperous life. Never let go of loyalty and faithfulness. Tie them round your neck; write them on your heart. If you do this both God and man will be pleased with you.

Thought: What two things should we 'never let go of'?

Prayer: Help us to obey Your teaching, Lord, so that You will be pleased with us. Amen.

Day 5

Proverbs 3.5-7

Trust in the Lord with all your heart. Never rely on what you think you know. Remember the Lord in everything you do, and he will show you the right way. Never let yourself think you are wiser than you are; simply obey the Lord and refuse to do wrong.

Thought: Do you find the 'two-part rule' in verse 7 hard or easy?

Prayer: Heavenly Father, when we have to make a choice between two courses of action, please show us the right way. Amen.

Day 6

Proverbs 3.9-10

Honour the Lord by making him an offering from the best of all that your land produces. If you do, your barns will be filled with grain, and you will have too much wine to be able to store it all.

Thought: Do we give God the first and best or what is left over?

Prayer: Forgive us, Lord, when we only give You what is left over from our money, our time and our energies, and help us to put You first. Amen.

Day 7

Proverbs 4.10-12
Listen to me, my son. Take seriously what I am telling you, and you will live a long life. I have taught you wisdom and the right way to live. Nothing will stand in your way if you walk wisely, and you will not stumble when you run.

Thought: it is a big responsibility to teach the young.

Prayer: Father God, help adults to teach young people by their behaviour as well as their words, and help the young to listen and to learn. Amen.

Week 12

Proverbs 30.1-33 were written by a man called Agur.

Day 1

Proverbs 30.7-9

I ask you, God, to let me have two things before I die: keep me from lying, and let me neither rich nor poor. So give me only as much food as I need. If I have more, I might say that I do not need you. But if I am poor, I might steal and bring disgrace on my God.

Thought: Agur thought both poverty and riches could be dangerous. Why?

Prayer: Father in Heaven, please give us sufficient for our daily needs and protect us from the dangers of poverty or great riches. Amen.

Day 2

Proverbs 30.11

There are people who curse their fathers and do not show their appreciation for their mothers.

Thought: Do you really 'appreciate' your mother?

Prayer: Show us today, Lord, something that we can do to show that we appreciate our mothers, and, if we have not got a mother, help us to think of something that will bring pleasure to a mother who never feels she is appreciated. Amen.

Day 3

Proverbs 30.12-14

There are people who think they are pure when they are as filthy as they can be.

There are people who think they are good - oh, how good they think they are!

There are people who take cruel advantage of the poor and needy; that is the way they make their living.'

Thought: Do you think you are *good*?

Prayer: Dear Father in Heaven, we confess that we continually fail to live up to Your standards. Please forgive us, and strengthen us as we try to live Your way. Amen.

Day 4

Proverbs 30.32-3

If you have been foolish enough to be arrogant and plan evil, stop and think! If you churn milk, you get butter. If you hit someone's nose, it bleeds. If you stir up anger, you get into trouble.'

Thought: STOP and THINK!

Prayer: Dear Lord Jesus, so much trouble occurs just because we do not stop and think about the consequences of our words or actions. Remind us today to STOP and THINK before we speak or act. Amen.

Day 5

Proverbs 31.8-9

'Speak up for people who cannot speak for themselves. Protect the rights of all who are helpless. Speak for them and be a righteous judge. Protect the rights of the poor and needy.'

Thought: Who should we protect and 'speak up for'?

Prayer: Father God, help us to keep our eyes and ears open for those who need our protection and someone to speak up for them. We pray today, too, for those whose job it is to protect the rights of others. Help them to do so with energy and conviction. Amen.

Day 6

Proverbs 23.12-15

Pay attention to your teacher and learn all you can.

Don't hesitate to discipline a child. A good spanking won't kill him. As a matter of fact it may save his life.

Son, if you become wise, I will be very happy. I will be proud when I hear you speaking words of wisdom.

Thought: Are we always 'ready to learn'?

Prayer: Almighty God, today we pray for all those who teach in schools, colleges and churches (especially . . .). Help those who learn to pay attention so that they may become wise about the things that really matter. Amen.

Day 7

Proverbs 23.22-5

Listen to your father; without him you would not exist. When your mother is old, show her your appreciation.

Truth, wisdom, learning, and good sense - these are worth paying for, but too valuable for you to sell.

A righteous man's father has good reason to be happy. You can take pride in a wise son.

Make your father and mother proud of you; give your mother that happiness.

Thought: What is 'worth paying for but too valuable to sell'?

Prayer: Dear Father in Heaven, give us the gifts of truth, wisdom, learning and good sense, and make our parents proud of us. Amen.

Week 13

*The word 'Genesis' means origin or starting point.
For the next three weeks we are going to read the Bible's account of
the creation of the universe and the creatures in it,
and the beginning of sin in the world.*

Day 1

Genesis 1.1-5

In the beginning, when God created the universe, the earth was formless
and desolate. The raging ocean that covered everything was engulfed in
total darkness, and the power of God was moving over the water. Then
God commanded, 'Let there be light' - and light appeared. God was
pleased with what he saw. Then he separated the light from the darkness,
and he named the light 'Day' and the darkness 'Night'. Evening passed
and morning came - that was the first day.

Thought: The world would be a dark place without God.

Prayer: We thank You, God, for the sun which lights the world and coaxes
living things into healthy growth. Amen.

Day 2

Genesis 1.6-8

Then God commanded, 'Let there be a dome to divide the water and to
keep it in two separate places' - and it was done. So God made a dome,
and it separated the water under it from the water above it. He named the
dome 'Sky.' Evening passed and morning came - that was the second day.

Thought: They sky is everywhere - so is God.

Prayer: Dear Father, as we look at the sky above us and breathe the air
around us, remind us that You are around us and within us all the time.
Amen.

Day 3

Genesis 1.9-13

Then God commanded, 'Let the water below the sky come together in
one place, so that the land will appear' - and it was done. He named the
land 'Earth,' and the water which had come together he named 'Sea.' And
God was pleased with what he saw. Then he commanded, 'Let the earth
produce all kinds of plants, those that bear grain and those that bear fruit'

- and it was done. So the earth produced all kinds of plants, and God was pleased with what he saw. Evening passed and morning came - that was the third day.

Thought: Variety's the very spice of life,
That gives it all its flavour.

William Cowper (1731-1800)

Do you agree?

Prayer: Almighty God, thank You for the plants, flowers and trees that You have given us to enjoy. We marvel at their infinite variety and praise You for Your creative power. Amen.

Day 4

Genesis 1.14-16
Then God commanded, 'Let lights appear in the sky to separate day from night and to show the time when days, years, and religious festivals begin; they will shine in the sky to give light to the earth' - and it was done. So God made the two larger lights, the sun to rule over the day and the moon to rule over the night; he also made the stars.

Thought: God made things to last!

Prayer: Dear God, You create things of lasting worth and beauty. In the 'throw-away' world in which we live give us some of Your creative power to make, and to do, things that are of lasting worth. Amen.

Day 5

Genesis 1.20-3
Then God commanded, 'Let the water be filled with many kinds of living beings, and let the air be filled with birds.' So God created the great sea-monsters, all kinds of creatures that live in the water, and all kinds of birds. And God was pleased with what he saw. He blessed them all and told the creatures that live in the water to reproduce, and to fill the sea, and he told the birds to increase in number. Evening passed and morning came - that was the fifth day.

Thought: God created and we are destroying.

Prayer: Father, forgive us for spoiling and polluting Your world, so that its creatures can no longer survive. Please be with all those who are working to put things right. Amen.

Day 6

Genesis 1.24-5

Then God commanded, 'Let the earth produce all kinds of animal life: domestic and wild, large and small' - and it was done. So God made them all, and he was pleased with what he saw.

Thought: Animals are God's creatures.

Prayer: Lord, we pray today, that You may bless all those who work with animals, striving to relieve and prevent their suffering. Help us to treat our own pets with care and consideration. Amen.

Day 7

Genesis 1.26-8

Then God said, 'And now we will make human beings; they will be like us and resemble us. They will have power over the fish, the birds, and all animals, domestic and wild, large and small.' So God created human beings, making them to be like himself. He created them male and female, blessed them, and said, 'Have many children, so that your descendants will live all over the earth and bring it under their control. I am putting you in charge of the fish, the birds, and all the wild animals.'

Thought: Being 'in charge' is a big responsibility!

Prayer: Father, You have given us power over fish, birds and all animals, domestic and wild. Forgive us for betraying Your trust, and show us today how we, as individuals, can use our power wisely, and for the benefit of Your creatures. Amen.

Week 14

Day 1

Genesis 2.1-4

And so the whole universe was completed. By the seventh day God finished what he had been doing and stopped working. He blessed the seventh day and set it apart as a special day, because by that day he had completed his creation and stopped working. And that is how the universe was created.

Thought: We all need time set apart - when we stop working.

Prayer: In our busy lives, please help us, Lord, to set apart a time when we follow Your example, stop working, and have time to think. Amen.

Day 2

Genesis 2.7-9

Then the Lord God took some soil from the ground and formed a man out of it; he breathed life-giving breath into his nostrils and the man began to live.

Then the Lord God planted a garden in Eden, in the East, and there he put the man he had formed. He made all kinds of beautiful trees grow there and produce good fruit. In the middle of the garden stood the tree that gives life and the tree that gives knowledge of what is good and what is bad.

Thought: God has put you in the place you are.

Prayer: Dear Father God, I believe that I am where I am because You have put me here. Help me to stay here and work for You, until you make clear that You want me to be somewhere else. Amen.

Day 3

Genesis 2.15-17

Then the Lord God placed the man in the Garden of Eden to cultivate it and guard it. He said to him, 'You may eat the fruit of any tree in the garden, except the tree that gives knowledge of what is good and what is bad. You must not eat the fruit of that tree; if you do, you will die the same day.'

Thought: When God forbids - it is for a good reason!

Prayer: Almighty God, we know that Your rules are made for man's good. Direct us clearly through Your Holy Spirit, so that we can clearly discern what is good and right and what is bad and wrong. Amen.

Day 4

Genesis 2.18-20
Then the Lord God said, 'It is not good for the man to live alone. I will make a suitable companion to help him.' So he took some soil from the ground and formed all the animals and all the birds. Then he brought them to the man to see what he would name them; and that is how they all got their names. So the man named all the birds and all the animals; but not one of them was a suitable companion to help him.

Thought: God has always sought man's co-operation.

Prayer: Almighty God, who sought man's help in naming the creatures of the world. Show us how we can share in Your work today. Amen.

Day 5

Genesis 2.21-2
Then the Lord God made the man fall into a deep sleep, and while he was sleeping, he took out one of the man's ribs and closed up the flesh. He formed a woman out of the rib and brought her to him.

Thought: The best relationships are those in which God has had a part in bringing a man and a woman together.

Prayer: Dear Father God, we think today of marriages where it seems obvious that You have drawn the partners together (especially . . .). Grant that their relationships may grow in love, trust and mutual comfort based on their love for You. Amen.

Day 6

Genesis 2.23-4
Then the man said,
   'At last, here is one of my own kind -
  Bone taken from my bone, and flesh from my flesh.
  "Woman" is her name because she was taken out of man.'
   That is why a man leaves his father and mother and is united with his wife, and they become one.

Thought: 'Leaving' is often a necessary part of a new beginning.

Prayer: Heavenly Father, You know that leaving familiar people and places is often hard for us; but when we are sure of Your leading, give us the courage to do it. Amen.

Day 7

Genesis 3.1-3

Now the snake was the most cunning animal that the Lord God had made. The snake asked the woman, 'Did God really tell you not to eat fruit from any tree in the garden?'

'We may eat the fruit of any tree in the garden,' the woman answered, 'except the tree in the middle of it. God told us not to eat of that tree or even touch it; if we do, we will die.'

Thought: Satan always tries to make us dissatisfied with what we have.

Prayer: We pray today, Father, for contentment. Thank You for everything You have given us. We thank You particularly for . . . Please save us from the sin of always wanting what we have not got. Amen.

Week 15

Day 1

Genesis 3.4-5

The snake replied. 'That's not true; you will not die. God said that, because he knows that when you eat it you will be like God and know what is good and what is bad.'

Thought: Unbelievers will always try to convince us that God does not mean what He says!

Prayer: Lord, when people say 'that's not true' about the Bible, prayer, or our Christian faith, help us to hold fast to our beliefs. Amen.

Day 2

Genesis 3.6-7

The woman saw how beautiful the tree was and how good its fruit would be to eat, and she thought how wonderful it would be to become wise. So she took some of the fruit and ate it. Then she gave some to her husband, and he also ate it. As soon as they had eaten it, they were given understanding and realised that they were naked; so they sewed fig leaves together and covered themselves.

Thought When we 'fall' we often cause others to stumble.

Prayer: O God, we know that when we are disobedient we often cause someone else to do wrong. Help us to remember this and to set a good example. Amen.

Day 3

Genesis 3.8

That evening they heard the Lord God walking in the garden, and they hid from him among the trees.

Thought: What do you think made Adam and Eve hide from God?

Prayer: Father, give us the courage to come to You when we have done wrong and not to try and hide from You, because when we seek and gain Your forgiveness, we know that we can put the past behind us. Amen.

Day 4

Genesis 3.9-11

But the Lord God called out to the man, 'Where are you?'

He answered, 'I heard you in the garden; I was afraid and hid from you, because I was naked.'

'Who told you that you were naked?' God asked. 'Did you eat the fruit that I told you not to eat?'

Thought: God encourages us to confess our sins fully and frankly.

Prayer: Lord, help us to confess our sins openly and fully to You, without excuses, knowing that You are only too ready to forgive those who are really sorry. Amen.

Day 5

Genesis 3.12-13

The man answered, 'The woman you put here with me gave me the fruit, and I ate it.'

The Lord God asked the woman, 'Why did you do this?'

She replied, 'The snake tricked me into eating it.'

Thought: How did Adam and Eve try to excuse themselves? Do you do this?

Prayer: Lord, we confess that we often do wrong things for which no one is to blame but ourselves; and yet we try to pass the blame on to other people. Forgive us, we pray You. Amen.

Day 6

Genesis 3.22-4

Then the Lord God said, 'Now the man has become like one of us and has knowledge of what is good and what is bad. He must not be allowed to eat fruit from the tree of life, and live for ever.' So the Lord God sent him out of the Garden of Eden and made him cultivate the soil from which he had been formed.

Thought: We *do* know what is good and what is bad - even when we claim that we do not!

Prayer: Heavenly Father, You have given to each one of us, however young or small, a knowledge of good and bad; may our wrong actions never separate us from You. Amen.

When you are beginning a book do you sometimes turn to the end
to reassure yourself that it has a happy ending?
We are going to do that today.

Day 7

Revelation 22.1-4
The angel also showed me the river of the water of life, sparkling like crystal, and coming from the throne of God and of the Lamb and flowing down the middle of the city's street. On each side of the river was the tree of life, which bears fruit twelve times a year, once each month; and its leaves are for the healing of the nations. Nothing that is under God's curse will be found in the city.

The throne of God and of the Lamb will be in the city, and his servants will worship him. They will see his face, and his name will be written on the foreheads.

Thought: It is not the beginning nor the end of our lives that is important, but what we do with the years in between!

Prayer: Lord, we know that You are wise and loving, and see the end of all things from the beginning; help us to walk in Your ways and listen to Your voice all the days of our lives. Amen.

Week 16

Timothy was a young Christian who became a companion and assistant to the Apostle Paul. For the next two weeks we are going to read parts of a letter written by Paul to Timothy, giving him some practical advice.

Day 1

1 Timothy 1.12-13

I give thanks to Christ Jesus our Lord, who has given me strength for my work. I thank him for considering me worthy and appointing me to serve him, even though in the past I spoke evil of him and persecuted and insulted him. But God was merciful to me because I did not yet have faith and so did not know what I was doing.

Thought: Our past is forgiven and forgotten by God.

Prayer: Father God, we thank You for forgiving the wrong things we did in the past (especially . . .) and for giving us a new beginning. Help us to serve You faithfully, today and every day. Amen.

Day 2

1 Timothy 1.15-16

This is a true saying, to be completely accepted and believed: Christ Jesus came into the world to save sinners. I am the worst of them, but God was merciful to me in order that Christ Jesus might show his full patience in dealing with me, the worst of sinners, as an example for all those who would later believe in him and receive eternal life.

Thought: Realising we are *bad* is healthier than thinking we are *good*!

Prayer: Dear Lord Jesus, thank You for coming into the world to save sinners like me, and for Your patience in dealing with me.Please use me to help others to believe in You and have eternal life. Amen.

Day 3

1 Timothy 1.18-19

Timothy, my child, I entrust to you this command, which is in accordance with the words of prophecy spoken in the past about you. Use these words as weapons in order to fight well, and keep your faith and a clear conscience. Some men have not listened to their conscience and have made a ruin of their faith.

Thought: Good advice! 'Keep your faith and a clear conscience!'

Prayer: Heavenly Father, give us a tender conscience that helps us to know if we are doing right or wrong, and a strong faith that enables us to trust in You, whatever the circumstances. Amen.

Day 4

1 Timothy 2.1-2
First of all, then, I urge that petitions, prayers, requests, and thanksgivings be offered to God for all people; for kings and all others who are in authority, that we may live a quiet and peaceful life with all reverence towards God and with proper conduct.

Thought: Rulers have cares as well as you and me!

Prayer: We pray today for all those in authority (especially . . .). Guide them in their decisions, give them clear minds when they are confused, and courage to speak out in defence of what they believe to be right; so that we may be enabled to live quiet and peaceful lives, with reverence towards God and proper conduct. Amen.

Day 5

1 Timothy 2.8
In every church service I want the men to pray, men who are dedicated to God and can lift up their hands in prayer without anger or argument.

Thought: 'I want the MEN to pray.'

Prayer: Lord, we pray today for Christian men (especially . . .). You intend them to take a leading part in the affairs of their homes and their churches. Help them to be dedicated to Your service, and to set an example by their prayers and peaceful behaviour. Amen.

Day 6

1 Timothy 2.9-10
I also want the women to be modest and sensible about their clothes and to dress properly; not with fancy hair styles or with gold ornaments or pearls or expensive dresses, but with good deeds, as is proper for women who claim to be religious.

Thought: 'Dress properly . . . with good deeds.'

Prayer: Dear Father God, You know that most of us like to dress well, and we spend quite a lot of time and money on clothes; help us to be modest and sensible in our dress, and also to be concerned with good deeds which never wear out or go out of fashion. Amen.

Day 7

1 Timothy 3.1-4

This is a true saying: If a man is eager to be a church leader, he desires an excellent work. A church leader must be without fault; he must have only one wife, be sober, self-controlled, and orderly; he must welcome strangers in his home; he must be able to teach; he must not be a drunkard or a violent man, but gentle and peaceful; he must not love money; he must be able to manage his own family well and make his children obey him with all respect.

Thought: High callings demand high standards!

Prayer: Almighty God, we pray today for our Church leaders; for Bishops, Ministers, Evangelists, and Lay people who are in positions of responsibility (especially our own . . .). Help them to live up to the high standards of their calling; forgive them when they fall, and give them patience and understanding for those they deal with. Amen.

Week 17

Day 1

1 Timothy 3.8-10

Church helpers must also have a good character and be sincere; they must not drink too much wine or be greedy for money; they should hold to the revealed truth of the faith with a clear conscience. They should be tested first, and then, if they pass the test, they are to serve.

Thought: 'Church helpers . . . should be tested . . . '

Prayer: Lord, give us wisdom to choose the right people to serve in our Church, so that we look for sincere people, of good character, who truly believe in You. Amen.

Day 2

1 Timothy 3.11-13

Their wives also must be of good character and must not gossip; they must be sober and honest in everything. A church helper must have only one wife, and be able to manage his children and family well. Those helpers who do their work well win for themselves a good standing and are able to speak boldly about their faith in Christ Jesus.

Thought: 'Wives also must be good character and must not gossip, they must be sober and honest in everything.'

Prayer: Dear Father God, we thank You today for the wives of Church Ministers and officials, who share in their husband's work and open their homes, often without thanks or recognition (especially . . .). Remind us to encourage them in their work and show that we appreciate them. Amen.

Day 3

1 Timothy 6.6-8

Well, religion does make a person very rich, if he is satisfied with what he has. What did we bring into the world? Nothing! What can we take out of the world? Nothing! So then, if we have enough food and clothes, that should be enough for us.

Thought: Are 'food and clothes' enough for us?

Prayer: Dear Lord Jesus, we pray today for contentment, and thank You for food, and clothes, and a home, and many blessings beside; knowing that many other people are cold, hungry, and homeless. Show us a practical way in which we can share all that we have. For Your dear sake. Amen.

Day 4

1 Timothy 6.9-10
But those who want to get rich fall into temptation and are caught in the trap of many foolish and harmful desires, which pull them down to ruin and destruction. For the love of money is a source of all kinds of evil. Some have been so eager to have it that they have wandered away from the faith and have broken their hearts with many sorrows.

Thought: 'Money is like muck - not good except it be spread!'
Francis Bacon (1561-1628)

Prayer: Lord, sometimes we wish that we had more money (to buy . . .). But we know in our hearts that money does not always bring happiness. Please help us to use what we have in the right way, and not to be constantly longing for things we do not have. Amen.

Day 5

1 Timothy 6.11-12
But you, man of God, avoid all these things. Strive for righteousness, godliness, faith, love, endurance, and gentleness. Run your best in the race of faith, and win eternal life for yourself; for it was to this life that God called you when you firmly professed your faith before many witnesses.

Thought: Are you a competitor or a spectator in the race of faith?

Prayer: Lord, make us all 'citizens' of God; help us to be good, faithful, loving and gentle, and not to give up when the going is hard, because this is the life to which You have called us. Amen.

Day 6

1 Timothy 6.17-19
Command those who are rich in the things of this life not to be proud, but to place their hope, not in such an uncertain thing as riches, but in God, who generously gives us everything for our enjoyment. Command them to do good, to be rich in good works, to be generous and ready to share with others. In this way they will store up for themselves a treasure which will be a solid foundation for the future. And then they will be able to win the life which is true life.

Thought: You double what you have when you give it away, and halve it when you keep it!

Prayer: Lord, the more we have, the more we can give away. Teach us the joy of being generous and sharing with others, which brings its own reward. Amen.

Day 7

1 Timothy 6.20-1
Timothy, keep safe what has been entrusted to your care. Avoid the profane talk and foolish arguments of what some people wrongly call 'Knowledge.' For some have claimed to possess it, and as a result they have lost the way of faith.

God's grace be with you all.

Thought: 'Avoid foolish arguments . . . '

Prayer: Heavenly Father, You know we sometimes argue and quarrel about things that really do not matter. Teach us to use our energy in holding fast to our faith, and to keep safe the really important things that have been entrusted to our care. Amen.

Week 18

*The book of Jonah is the story of a man who tried to disobey God.
God sent him to take a message of warning to the city of Nineveh but
Johah did not want to go, so he set off in the opposite direction!
We will see what happened!*

Day 1

Jonah 1.1-3

One day, the Lord spoke to Jonah son of Amittai. He said 'Go to Nineveh,
that great city, and speak out against it; I am aware how wicked its people
are.' Jonah, however, set out in the opposite direction in order to get away
from the Lord. He went to Joppa, where he found a ship about to go to
Spain. He paid his fare and went aboard with the crew to sail to Spain,
where he would be away from the Lord.

Thought: Do you sometimes disobey God and set out 'in the opposite
direction'?

Prayer: Dear God, we confess that sometimes our wishes clash with what
we know to be Your will. Help us not to run away from the place You wish
us to be. Amen.

Day 2

Jonah 1.4-5

But the Lord sent a strong wind on the sea, and the storm was so violent
that the ship was in danger of breaking up. The sailors were terrified and
cried out for help, each one to his own god. Then, in order to lessen the
danger, they threw the cargo over-board. Meanwhile, Jonah had gone
below and was lying in the ship's hold, sound asleep.

Thought: Are we sometimes unaware that we have caused a 'storm'?

Prayer: Dear Lord, show us whenever we have been the cause of a 'storm'
in our home, our church, our school, or our work place, and help us to put
things right. Amen.

Day 3

Jonah 1.11-12, 15

The storm was getting worse all the time, so the sailors asked him, 'What
should we do to you to stop the storm?'

Jonah answered, 'Throw me into the sea, and it will calm down. I know it is my fault that you are caught in this violent storm.'

Then they picked Jonah up and threw him into the sea, and it calmed down at once.

Thought: Jonah took his punishment as Jesus took ours.

Prayer: Lord Jesus Christ, You took the punishment for our wrongdoing, so that we could be at peace with God, Thank you. Amen.

Day 4

Jonah 1.17; 2.1-2

At the Lord's command a large fish swallowed Jonah, and he was inside the fish for three days and nights.

From deep inside the fish Jonah prayed to the Lord his God:

'In my distress, O Lord, I called to you, and you answered me.'

Thought: We can pray to God at any time and in any place.

Prayer: Heavenly Father, we thank You that we can pray to You at any time and in any place, and that You will hear and answer our prayer. Amen.

Day 5

Jonah 2.10; 3.1-3

Then the Lord ordered the fish to spew Jonah up on the beach, and it did.

Once again the Lord spoke to Jonah. He said, 'Go to Nineveh, that great city, and proclaim to the people the message I have given you.' So Jonah obeyed the Lord and went to Nineveh . . .

Thought: God often gives us a second chance.

Prayer: Father God, we admit we often fail You; please give us a second chance to obey Your voice. Amen.

Day 6

Jonah 3.5, 10

The people of Nineveh believed God's message. So they decided that everyone should fast, and all the people, from the greatest to the least, put on sackcloth to show that they had repented.

God saw what they did; he saw that they had given up their wicked behaviour. So he changed his mind and did not punish them as he had said he would.

Thought: God is delighted to see us change our ways.

Prayer: Lord, we know that we often do things that make You unhappy. Please make us truly repentant and help us to give up our bad behaviour. Amen.

Day 7

Jonah 4.1, 4
Jonah was very unhappy about this and became angry.
  The Lord answered, 'What right have you to be angry . . . ?'

Thought: Do we dare to be less forgiving than God?

Prayer: Almighty God, we confess, with shame, that we sometimes feel that certain people do not deserve Your forgiveness for the wicked things they have done, and wish that You would withhold it. Give us loving hearts to pray for them. Amen.

Week 19

This letter was written by St Paul to prepare the way for a visit he planned to make to the Church at Rome. He wrote explaining the Christian faith and the effect that becoming a Christian would have on people' daily lives.

Day 1

Romans 2.6-8

For God will reward every person according to what he has done. Some people keep on doing good, and seek glory, honour, and immortal life; to them God will give eternal life. Other people are selfish and reject what is right, in order to follow what is wrong; on them God will pour out anger and fury.

Thought: Do you think it is fair to reward the good and punish the bad? If so, why?

Prayer: Dear Lord, help us to go on doing good in order to please You. Amen.

Day 2

Romans 5.6-8

For when we were still helpless, Christ died for the wicked at the time that God chose. It is a difficult thing for someone to die for a righteous person. It may even be that someone might dare to die for a good person. But God has shown us how much he loves us - it was while we were still sinners that Christ died for us!

Thought: If Christ died for us - we should want to live for Him.

Prayer: O Lord,
  Help us to serve Thee as Thou deservest,
  To give and not to count the cost,
  To fight and not to heed the wounds,
  To toil and not to seek for rest,
  To labour and to ask for no reward
  Save that of knowing that we do Thy will.
  Amen.

St Ignatius de Loyala (1491-1556)

Day 3

Romans 5.10-11

We were God's enemies, but he made us his friends through the death of his Son. Now that we are God's friends, how much more will we be saved by Christ's life! But that is not all; we rejoice because of what God has done through our Lord Jesus Christ, who has now made us God's friends.

Thought: Are you a 'friend' or an 'enemy' of God?

Prayer: Dear Lord Jesus, thank You for making it possible to become 'friends' with God, by taking the punishment for our wrongdoing. Amen.

Day 4

Romans 7.15, 24-5

I do not understand what I do; for I don't do what I would like to do, but instead I do what I hate . . . What an unhappy man I am! Who will rescue me from this body that is taking me to death? Thanks be to God, who does this through our Lord Jesus Christ!

This, then, is my condition: on my own I can serve God's law only with my mind, while my human nature serves the law of sin.

Thought: 'I don't do what I would like to do . . . I do what I hate!' Is this your experience?

Prayer: Lord Jesus, when good and evil fight together in our lives, give good the victory through Your strength we pray. Amen.

Day 5

Romans 8.14-16

Those who are led by God's Spirit are God's sons. For the Spirit that God has given you does not make you slaves and cause you to be afraid; instead, the Spirit makes you God's children, and by the Spirit's power we cry out to God, 'Father! my Father!' God's Spirit joins himself to our spirits to declare that we are God's children.

Thought: Do not be afraid to ask God for help.

Prayer: Father! my Father! We are your sons and daughters! We will not be afraid of anything that life can bring but we will put ourselves into Your hands. Amen.

Day 6

Romans 8.28

We know that in all things God works for good with those who love him, those whom he has called according to his purpose.

Thought: God can bring good out of everything.

Prayer: Father in Heaven, remind us that You are always watching over us and that our good is Your concern. Amen.

Day 7

Romans 12.11-13

Work hard and do not be lazy. Serve the Lord with a heart full of devotion. Let your hope keep you joyful, be patient in your troubles, and pray at all times. Share your belongings with your needy fellow-Christians, and open your homes to strangers.

Thought: Can you find the seven rules for happiness in these verses?

Prayer: Lord Jesus, help us to follow Your 'rule for happiness' and fill our lives with love for You and our Christian brothers and sisters. Amen.

Week 20

Day 1

Romans 12.14-16

Ask God to bless those who persecute you - yes, ask him to bless, not to curse. Be happy with those who are happy, weep with those who weep. Have the same concern for everyone. Do not be proud, but accept humble duties. Do not think of yourselves as wise.

Thought: Do you find it easier to share people's joys or their sorrows? Why?

Prayer: Lord, You know it is sometimes harder to share other people's joys, especially if they have been given something that we would like (i.e. promotion, a baby, a new home, a husband, a place in the team, a new car, a bicycle . . .). Help us to be unselfish and rejoice with them. Amen.

Day 2

Romans 12.17-19

If someone has done you wrong, do not repay him with a wrong. Try to do what everyone considers to be good. Do everything possible on your part to live in peace with everybody. Never take revenge, my friends, but instead let God's anger do it. For the scripture says, 'I will take revenge, I will pay back, says the Lord.'

Thought: Do we do everything possible to enable us to live at peace with everybody?

Prayer: Father in Heaven, You know that there are some people we find it hard to live and work with (especially . . .). Help us to do everything in our power to keep the peace. Amen.

Day 3

Romans 13.3-4

For rulers are not to be feared by those who do good, but by those who do evil. Would you like to be unafraid of the man in authority? Then do what is good, and he will praise you, because he is God's servant working for your own good. But if you do evil, then be afraid of him, because his power to punish is real. He is God's servant and carries out God's punishment on those who do evil.

Thought: Man's laws are often God-made.

Prayer: Lord, help us to keep the laws of our country (. . . the rules of our school or workplace . . .), but help us, above all, to be obedient to You. Amen.

Day 4

Romans 13.5-7

For this reason you must obey the authorities - not just because of God's punishment, but also as a matter of conscience.

That is also why you pay taxes, because the authorities are working for God when they fulfil their duties. Pay, then, what you owe them; pay them your personal and property taxes, and show respect and honour for them all.

Thought: A new way of looking at income tax inspectors!

Prayer: Almighty God, we pray today for all those whose job it is to administer the law; judges, policemen, traffic wardens, and those in other official positions. Give them wisdom and a sensitive conscience to do what is right and just. Amen.

Day 5

Romans 13.8, 10

Be under obligation to no one - the only obligation you have is to love one another. Whoever does this has obeyed the Law . . . If you love someone, you will never do him wrong; to love, then, is to obey the whole Law.

Thought: What is our 'only obligation'?

Prayer: Lord, we know that loving people may be easy, but it can sometimes be very hard when they behave in an unloving way towards us. Teach us to love people whole-heartedly - whatever they do - as You love us. Amen.

Day 6

Romans 13.12

The night is nearly over, day is almost here. Let us stop doing the things that belong to the dark, and let us take up weapons for fighting in the light.

Thought: Time is running out!

Prayer: Remind us, Lord, that each day brings Your Second Coming nearer, and help us to live as people of the light. Amen.

Day 7

Romans 14.1, 4

Welcome the person who is weak in faith, but do not argue with him about his personal opinions . . . Who are you to judge the servant of someone else? It is his own Master who will decide whether he succeeds or fails. And he will succeed, because the Lord is able to make him succeed.

Thought: We are not *always* right!

Prayer: Lord, help us to understand that there are many paths that lead to You, and that *our* way is not necessarily the only one. Amen.

Week 21

Day 1

Romans 14.10, 12

You then, who eat only vegetables - why do you pass judgement on your brother? And you who eat anything - why do you despise your brother? All of us will stand before God to be judged by him . . .

Every one of us, then, will have to give an account of himself to God.

Thought: Let us keep criticism for ourselves.

Prayer: Dear God, teach us to make excuses and allowances for others, and help us to stop making excuses and allowances for ourselves. Amen.

Day 2

Romans 14.13

So . . . let us stop judging one another. Instead, you should decide never to do anything that would make your brother stumble or fall into sin.

Thought: Do you ever cause someone to 'stumble' by your behaviour?

Prayer: Father, help us to remember that our behaviour can either help or hinder other people. Amen.

Day 3

Romans 14.20-1

Do not, because of food, destroy what God has done. All foods may be eaten, but it is wrong to eat anything that will cause someone else to fall into sin. The right thing to do is to keep from eating meat, drinking wine, or doing anything else that will make your brother fall.

Thought: What is our attitude towards vegetarians or teetotallers?

Prayer: Dear Father God, please help us to be tolerant and helpful towards people with strong convictions, even though we may not share them. Amen.

Day 4

Romans 15.1-2

We who are strong in the faith ought to help the weak to carry their burdens. We should not please ourselves. Instead, we should all please our brothers for their own good, in order to build them up in one faith.

Thought: What kind of 'burdens' can we help to carry?

Prayer: Dear Lord, bring to our minds today the name of someone who has a 'burden' and show us how we can help them to carry it. Amen.

Day 5

Romans 16.17-18

I urge you, my brothers: watch out for those who cause divisions and upset people's faith and go against the teaching which you have received. Keep away from them! For those who do such things are not serving Christ our Lord, but their own appetites. By their fine words and flattering speech they deceive innocent people.

Thought: Every Church has its trouble makers!

Prayer: Father in Heaven, sometimes there are arguments and upsets in our church . . . (especially about . . .). Help us not to get personally involved, unless it is in the role of peace-maker. Amen.

Day 6

Romans 16.19

Everyone has heard of your loyalty to the gospel, and for this reason I am happy about you. I want you to be wise about what is good, but innocent in what is evil.

Thought: What made Paul happy?

Prayer: Lord, make us wise about what is good and innocent of all that is evil, and may Your grace be with us always. Amen.

Day 7

Romans 16.25-6

Let us give glory to God! He is able to make you stand firm in your faith, according to the Good News I preach about Jesus Christ and according to the revelation of the secret truth which was hidden for long ages in the past. Now, however, that truth has been brought out into the open through the writings of the prophets; and by the command of the eternal God it is made known to all nations, so that all may believe and obey.

Thought: How has the truth about Jesus been 'brought out into the open'?

Prayer: Lord Jesus, we thank You that the truth about You is here, in writing, for us to read. Help us to continue to read and understand it, and act upon it. Amen.

Week 22

For the next four weeks we are going to read from the book of Esther, in the Old Testament. This is the story of a young Jewish girl, who by her courage and devotion to her people, saved them from being destroyed by their enemies.

Day 1

Esther 1.1-4
From his royal throne in Persia's capital city of Susa, King Xerxes ruled over 127 provinces, all the way from India to Sudan. In the third year of his reign he gave a banquet for all his officials and administrators. The armies of Persia and Media were present, as well as the governors and noblemen of the provinces. For six whole months he made a show of the riches of the imperial court with all its splendour and majesty.

Thought: Do we like to show off our possessions?

Prayer: Dear Father God, forgive us when we see our possessions as symbols of our own importance instead of gifts from You, intended to be used for the good of others. Amen.

Day 2

Esther 1.5
After that, the king gave a banquet for all the men in the capital city of Susa, rich and poor alike. It lasted a whole week and was held in the gardens of the royal palace.

Thought: 'The king gave a banquet . . . for rich and poor alike . . . '

Prayer: Dear Lord Jesus, next time we give a party, or ask people round for coffee or a meal, help us to consult You before we decide whom to invite. Amen.

Day 3

Esther 1.6
The courtyard there was decorated with blue and white cotton curtains, tied by cords of fine purple linen to silver rings on marble columns. Couches made of gold and silver had been placed in the courtyard, which was paved with white marble, red feldspar, shining mother-of-pearl, and blue turquoise.

Thought: How much of *our* money is spent on luxuries?

Prayer: Lord, help us through our prayers to plan our spending, and not to forget those of our brothers and sisters who have not enough to eat or drink, and who are cold, homeless or sick. Amen.

Day 4

Esther 1.7-8

Drinks were served in gold cups, no two of them alike, and the king was generous with the royal wine. There were no limits on the drinks; the king had given orders to the palace servants that everyone could have as much as he wanted.

Thought: No limit on the drinks! Good or bad?

Prayer: Almighty God, teach us to limit our appetites for food, drink, clothes and furniture, houses, holidays, toys (or any other material thing), so that we can enjoy all the good things You have provided, without becoming greedy or extravagant. Amen.

Day 5

Esther 1.9, 11-12

Meanwhile, inside the royal palace, Queen Vashti was giving a banquet for the women . . . He [the king] ordered them to bring in Queen Vashti, wearing her royal crown. The queen was a beautiful woman, and the king wanted to show off her beauty to the officials and all his guests. But when the servants told Queen Vashti of the king's command, she refused to come. This made the king furious.

Thought: Was the Queen right or wrong when she refused to come?

Prayer: Heavenly Father, give us the courage to say 'No' when we are asked to do something which we feel to be wrong. Amen.

Day 6

Esther 1.13, 16

Now it was the king's custom to ask for expert opinion on questions of law and order, so he called for his advisers, who would know what should be done . . .

Then Memucan declared to the king and his officials: 'Queen Vashti has insulted not only the king but also his officials - in fact, every man in the empire!'

Thought: We need to choose carefully whom we ask for good advice!

Prayer: Dear God, when someone gives us advice, teach us to match it against Your teaching, before we accept it. Amen.

Day 7

Esther 1.19, 21

'If it please Your Majesty, issue a royal proclamation that Vashti may never again appear before the king. Order it to be written into the laws of Persia and Media, so that it can never be changed. Then give her place as queen to some better woman.'

The king and his officials liked this idea, and the king did what Memucan suggested.

Thought: ' . . . I [God] do not judge as man judges. Man looks at the outward appearance, but I look at the heart.' (1 Samuel 16.7)

Do you think the queen deserved this severe sentence?

Prayer: Loving Heavenly Father, sometimes we are misjudged and accused of something of which we are innocent. Comfort us with the knowledge that You know the truth of all matters. Amen.

Week 23

Day 1

Esther 2.1-2, 4

Later, even after the king's anger had cooled down, he kept thinking about what Vashti had done and about his proclamation against her. So some of the king's advisers who were close to him suggested, 'Why don't you make a search to find some beautiful young virgins? . . . Then take the girl you like best and make her queen in Vashti's place.'

Thought: What we want to hear often seems to us to be good advice!

Prayer: Lord, when we require good and sound advice remind us to lay the matter before You and to wait patiently until Your Holy Spirit speaks to our heart and tells us what to do. Amen.

Day 2

Esther 2.5, 7

There in Susa lived a Jew named Mordecai son of Jair; he was from the tribe of Benjamin and was a descendant of Kish and Shimei . . . He had a cousin, Esther, whose Hebrew name was Hadassah; she was a beautiful girl, and had a good figure. At the death of her parents, Mordecai had adopted her and brought her up as his own daughter.

Thought: Do we care about those whose parents have died?

Prayer: Father in Heaven, thank You for those who spend their lives caring for fatherless and motherless children. Show us any way in which we can encourage them and help them in their work. Amen.

Day 3

Esther 2.8, 10-11

When the king had issued his new proclamation and many girls were being brought to Susa, Esther was among them. She too was put in the royal palace in the care of Hegai, who had charge of the harem.

Now, on the advice of Mordecai, Esther had kept it secret that she was Jewish. Every day Mordecai would walk to and fro in front of the courtyard of the harem, in order to find out how she was getting on and what was going to happen to her.

Thought: We should 'keep in touch' with our relations.

Prayer: Lord Jesus, help us to care about our relations and friends (especially . . .), and to write to them or telephone and visit them in order to find out how they are getting on. Amen.

Day 4

Esther 2.15, 17

The time came for Esther to go to the king. Esther - the daughter of Abihail and the cousin of Mordecai, who had adopted her as his daughter; Esther - admired by everyone who saw her. When her turn came, she wore just what Hegai, the eunuch in charge of the harem, advised her to wear.

The king liked her more than any of the other girls, and more than any of the others she won his favour and affection. He placed the royal crown on her head and made her queen in place of Vashti.

Thought: Even important people can be easily replaced!

Prayer: Dear Lord, we are sometimes tempted to think that we are indispensable. Keep us humble, and remind us how easily we can be replaced. Amen.

Day 5

Esther 2.19-20

Meanwhile Mordecai had been appointed by the king to an administrative position. As for Esther, she had still not let it be known that she was Jewish. Mordecai had told her not to tell anyone, and she obeyed him in this, just as she had obeyed him when she was a little girl under his care.

Thought: Do you think it was wrong of Mordecai to swear Esther to secrecy over her nationality?

Prayer: Lord Jesus, please give great wisdom to those who have to choose between telling the truth and being unjustly penalised, and concealing information that might get them into trouble. Amen.

Day 6

Esther 3.1-2, 5-6

Some time later King Xerxes promoted a man named Haman to the position of prime minister . . . The king ordered all the officials in his service to show their respect for Haman by kneeling and bowing to him. They all did so, except for Mordecai, who refused to do it . . . Haman was furious when he realised that Mordecai was not going to kneel and bow to him, and when he learnt that Mordecai was a Jew, he decided to do more than punish Mordecai alone. He made plans to kill every Jew in the whole Persian Empire.

Thought: Would promotion make *us* self-important or harsh?

Prayer: Almighty God, we pray today for those in high office, especially presidents, prime ministers, and others in authority. Help them to show wisdom, tact and modesty, and save them from the sin of self-importance. Amen.

Day 7

Esther 3.8-9

So Haman told the king, 'There is a certain race of people scattered all over your empire and found in every province. They observe customs that are not like those of any other people. Moreover, they do not obey the laws of the empire, so it is not in your best interests to tolerate them. If it please Your Majesty, issue a decree that they are to be put to death.'

Thought: 'They observe customs that are not like those of any other people.'
   Is this a fault?

Prayer: Lord, You have made us all different. Help us to understand other people who think, live, dress and behave, differently to ourselves, and teach us to rejoice in variety. Amen.

Week 24

Day 1

Esther 3.10-11

The king took off his ring, which was used to stamp proclamations and make them official, and gave it to the enemy of the Jewish people, Haman son of Hammedatha, the descendant of Agag. The king told him, 'The people and their money are yours; do as you like with them.'

Thought: If we 'do as we like' will God like what we do?

Prayer: Dear Father God, please guide us to use our authority, our influence and our resources, in a way that will improve the quality of the lives of our fellow men. Amen.

Day 2

Esther 3.12-13

So on the thirteenth day of the first month Haman called the king's secretaries and dictated a proclamation to be translated into every language and system of writing used in the empire and to be sent to all the rulers, governors, and officials. It was issued in the name of King Xerxes and stamped with his ring. Runners took this proclamation to every province of the empire. It contained the instructions that on a single day, the thirteenth day of Adar, all Jews - young and old, women and children - were to be killed.

Thought: At times when we can do nothing else, we can still pray.

Prayer: Lord, we pray today for those in prison and under sentence of death, because of the whim of a cruel and unjust ruler (especially . . .). Give them courage and strength in their ordeal, and if it be Thy will, a happy and hopeful future. Amen.

Day 3

Esther 4.1, 3

When Mordecai learnt of all that had been done, he tore his clothes in anguish. Then he dressed in sackcloth, covered his head with ashes, and walked through the city, wailing loudly and bitterly . . . Throughout all the provinces, wherever the king's proclamation was made known, there was loud mourning among the Jews. They fasted, wept and wailed, and most of them put on sackcloth and lay in ashes.

Thought: Hope can dispel despair.

Prayer: Lord Jesus, we pray today for those who mourn: for their country, for their freedom, for a loved one, or for their own wasted lives. Grant that our prayers may help to give them hope, and that their hope will motivate them into action. Amen.

Day 4

Esther 4.4, 5
When Esther's servant-girls and eunuchs told her what Mordecai was doing, she was deeply disturbed . . . Then she called Hathach, one of the palace eunuchs appointed as her servant by the king, and told him to go to Mordecai and find out what was happening and why.

Thought: Do we take the trouble to find out the cause of other people's unhappiness?

Prayer: Dear God, give us a real concern for people who are unhappy, and help us to relieve their sorrow when we can. Amen.

Day 5

Esther 4.12-14
When Mordecai received Esther's message, he sent her this warning: 'Don't imagine that you are safer than any other Jew just because you are in the royal palace. If you keep quiet at a time like this, help will come from heaven to the Jews, and they will be saved, but you will die and your father's family will come to an end. Yet who knows - maybe it was for a time like this that you were made queen!'

Thought: Are we sometimes tempted to 'keep quiet' when we should speak out?

Prayer: Lord, there are times we are tempted to keep quiet when we know we should speak out. Give us boldness and courage to say and do what is right. Amen.

Day 6

Esther 4.15-16
Esther sent Mordecai this reply: 'Go and gather all the Jews in Susa together; hold a fast and pray for me. Don't eat or drink anything for three days and nights. My servant-girls and I will be doing the same. After that, I will go to the king, even though it is against the law. If I must die for doing it, I will die.'

Thought: Prayer prepares.

Prayer: Almighty God, remind us to pray when we have something important to do for You, and remind us to pray for others, that You will give them wisdom, guidance and strength to do what is right, whatever it may cost them. Amen.

Day 7

Esther 5.1-3

On the third day of her fast Esther put on her royal robes and went and stood in the inner courtyard of the palace, facing the throne room. The king was inside, seated on the royal throne, facing the entrance. When the king saw Queen Esther standing outside, she won his favour, and he held out to her the gold sceptre. She then came up and touched the tip of it. 'What is it, Queen Esther?' the king asked. 'Tell me what you want, and you shall have it - even if it is half my empire.'

Thought: There is a right and a wrong way to approach those in authority!

Prayer: Dear God, when we approach those in authority in order to gain their support, give us guidance to do so with courtesy and tact. Amen.

Week 25

Day 1

Esther 5.4-5; 7.2

Esther replied, 'If it please Your Majesty, I would like you and Haman to be my guests tonight at a banquet I am preparing for you.'

The king then ordered Haman to come quickly, so that they could be Esther's guests. So the king and Haman went to Esther's banquet . . .

Over the wine the king asked her again, 'Now, Queen Esther, what do youwant? Tell me and you shall have it. I'll even give you half the empire.'

Thought: Do you ever make impulsive promises that you do not intend to keep?

Prayer: Lord, You know we sometimes make extravagant promises that are hard to keep. Help us only to promise those things that we intend to carry out. Amen.

Day 2

Esther 7.3-4

Queen Esther answered, 'If it please Your Majesty to grant my humble request, my wish is that I may live and that my people may live. My people and I have been sold for slaughter. If it were nothing more serious than being sold into slavery, I would have kept quiet and not bothered you about it; but we are about to be destroyed - exterminated!'

Thought: Queen Esther did not waste words!

Prayer: Lord Jesus, help us to use words carefully, in prayer, in conversation and in letters. Amen.

Day 3

Esther 7.5-7

Then King Xerxes asked Queen Esther, 'Who dares to do such a thing? Where is this man?'

Esther answered, 'Our enemy, our persecutor, is this evil man Haman!' Haman stared at the king and queen in terror. The king got up in a fury, left the room, and went outside to the palace gardens. Haman could see that the king was determined to punish him for this, so he stayed behind to beg Queen Esther for his life.

Thought: Man often demands judgement and punishment. Jesus taught forgiveness and mercy.

Paryer: Dear Lord Jesus, Who died to take the punishment for our sin, help us to be merciful in our judgement of others, and give us the ability to forgive. Amen.

Day 4

Esther 8.3-6

Then Esther spoke to the king again, throwing herself at his feet and crying. She begged him to do something to stop the evil plot that Haman, the descendant of Agag, had made against the Jews. The king held out the gold sceptre to her, so she stood up and said, 'If it please Your Majesty, and if you care about me and if it seems right to you, please issue a proclamation to prevent Haman's orders from being carried out - those orders that the son of Hammedatha the descendant of Agag gave for the destruction of all the Jews in the empire. How can I endure it if this disaster comes on my people, and my own relatives are killed?'

Thought: 'DO something!'

Prayer: Father, give us a real concern for our relatives (especially . . .), and help us to do all we can to ensure their happiness and well-being. Amen.

Day 5

Esther 8.7, 8

King Xerxes then said to Queen Esther and Mordecai, the Jew . . .
' . . . a proclamation issued in the king's name and stamped with the royal seal cannot be revoked. You may, however, write to the Jews whatever you wish; and you may write it in my name and stamp it with the royal seal.'

Thought: ALL the letters we write should be written in the name of Jesus and stamped 'with His seal'.

Prayer: Our Heavenly King, as we write letters, remind us that we, as Christians, write in Your name, and may they always be worthy to bear Your seal of approval. Amen.

Day 6

Esther 8.9, 11

Mordecai called the king's secretaries and dictated letters to the Jews These letters explained that the king would allow the Jews in every city to organise themselves for self-defence. If they were attacked by armed men of any nationality in any province, they [the Jews] could fight back and destroy them . . . '

Thought: The Jews could 'fight back' against the enemy - so can we!

Prayer: Lord, we confess we sometimes allow ourselves to be defeated by evil without fighting back (especially over things like . . .). Remind us that You are on our side and, if we claim your help, You will give us victory. Amen.

Day 7

Esther 8.15, 16, 17
Then the streets of Susa rang with cheers and joyful shouts. For the Jews there was joy and relief, happiness and a sense of victory. In every city and province, wherever the king's proclamation was read, the Jews held a joyful holiday with feasting and happiness . . .

Thought: 'Joy, relief, happiness, and a sense of victory!'

Prayer: Thank You, Lord, for giving all Christians the ability to win, with Your help, the important battle over sin and evil. May our happiness blossom into joy and relief and a sense of victory that will make others want to know more about You. Amen.

Final note:
The attack on the Jews, organised by the wicked Haman, resulted in considerable loss of life as the Jews turned in fury on those who would have destroyed them; but had it not been for Queen Esther's intervention the Jews in Persia would, have been completely wiped out. The story shows how one person, with the help of God, can be used to change the course of history. It also reminds us how difficult it can be to check a force of evil once unleashed.

Week 26

For the next three weeks we are going to 'dip in' to St. Paul's letter to the Church at Corinth - a large and important city in Greece.

Day 1

1 Corinthians 1.1-3

From Paul, who was called by the will of God to be an apostle of Christ Jesus, and from our brother Sosthenes -

To the church of God which is in Corinth, to all who are called to be God's holy people, who belong to him in union with Christ Jesus, together with all people everywhere, who worship our Lord Jesus Christ, their Lord and ours:

May God our Father and the Lord Jesus Christ give you grace and peace.

Thought: Substitute the name of your town for 'Corinth' in verse 2, and you can make these verses your own prayer for *your* church.

Day 2

1 Corinthians 1.4-5

I always give thanks to my God for you because of the grace he has given you through Christ Jesus. For in union with Christ you have become rich in all things, including all speech and all knowledge.

Thought: 'I always give thanks for you . . . '

Prayer: Dear Lord, we thank You today for . . . who sets us an example by the way they live and behave. Continue to bless them we ask You. Amen.

Day 3

1 Corinthians 1.6-8

The message about Christ has become so firmly established in you that you have not failed to receive a single blessing, as you wait for our Lord Jesus Christ to be revealed. He will also keep you firm to the end, so that you will be faultless on the Day of our Lord Jesus Christ. God is to be trusted, the God who called you to have fellowship with his Son Jesus Christ, our Lord.

Thought: 'He will keep you firm to the end.'

Prayer: Dear Father in Heaven, please keep us firm in our determination to follow You, and encourage us when we feel like giving up. Amen.

Day 4

1 Corinthians 1.26-7

Now remember what you were, my brothers, when God called you. From the human point of view few of you were wise or powerful or of high social standing. God purposely chose what the world considers nonsense in order to shame the wise, and he chose what the world considers weak in order to shame the powerful.

Thought: Do you think yourself wise and powerful or foolish and weak?

Prayer: Almighty God, thank you for making clear that we do not need to be wise or powerful or of high social standing in order to serve You. Take us just as we are and use us as You want to. Amen.

Day 5

1 Corinthians 1.29-31

This means that no one can boast in God's presence. But God has brought you into union with Christ Jesus, and God has made Christ to be our wisdom. By him we are put right with God; we become God's holy people and are set free. So then, as the scripture says, 'Whoever wants to boast must boast of what the Lord has done.'

Thought: How are we 'put right with God . . . and set free'?

Prayer: Dear Lord Jesus, thank You for continually forgiving us for the wrong things we do, and for taking our punishment upon Yourself when You died on the cross. Amen.

Day 6

1 Corinthians 3.9-10

For we are partners working together for God, and you are God's field.
    You are also God's building. Using the gift that God gave me, I did the work of an expert builder and laid the foundation, and another man is building on it. But each one must be careful how he builds.

Thought: Foundations are important!

Prayer: Please God remind us that each day we are adding to the building of our lives by what we say and do. Help us to build on firm foundations, and to Your glory. Amen.

Day 7

1 Corinthians 3.12-13

Some will use gold or silver or precious stones in building on the foundation; others will use wood or grass or straw. And the quality of each person's work will be seen when the Day of Christ exposes it. For on that Day fire will reveal everyone's work; the fire will test it and show its real quality.

Thought: Wood, grass, and straw burn easily!

Prayer: Lord, fill our minds and hearts and lives with things that are good and deserve praise; things that are true and noble; things that are right, pure, lovely and honourable; and help us to build our spiritual lives on the firm foundation of faith in You. Amen.

Week 27

Day 1

1 Corinthians 3.16
Surely you know that you are God's temple and that God's Spirit lives in you!

Thought: Do we treat our bodies as God's temple?

Prayer: Lord Jesus, Who lives within us and speaks through us; help us to keep our bodies and minds clean and wholesome so that we are a fit home for Your spirit. Amen.

Day 2

1 Corinthians 4.1-2
You should think of us as Christ's servants, who have been put in charge of God's secret truths. The one thing required of such a servant is that he be faithful to his master.

Thought: What is the 'one thing' required of a servant?

Prayer: Dear Father in Heaven, we want to be loyal and faithful servants. We promise we will try not to let You down by anything we do or say. Amen.

Day 3

1 Corinthians 4.3
Now, I am not at all concerned about being judged by you or by any human standard; I don't even pass judgement on myself.

Thought: God's approval is more important than other people's.

Prayer: Dear Father God, help us to aim to please You, and not to be so concerned about other people's opinion of us. Amen.

Day 4

1 Corinthians 4.4
My conscience is clear, but that does not prove that I am really innocent. The Lord is the one who passes judgement on me.

Thought: How reliable is *your* conscience?

Prayer: Almighty God, please give us a tender conscience, that encourages us do right and checks us when we would do wrong; but remind us that You are our only reliable guide. Amen.

Day 5

[1] Corinthians 4.5
So you should not pass judgement on anyone before the right time comes. Final judgement must wait until the Lord comes; he will bring to light the dark secrets and expose the hidden purposes of people's minds. And then everyone will receive from God the praise he deserves.

Thought: Have you any 'secret hidden purposes' which you prefer to keep 'in the dark'?

Prayer: Almighty God, Who knows all our dark secrets and hidden purposes, cause the light of Your forgiving love to shine in our hearts, so that our lives become clean and open. Amen.

Day 6

1 Corinthians 4.10-11
For Chirst's sake we are fools; but you are wise in union with Christ! We are weak, but you are strong! We are despised, but you are honoured! To this very moment we go hungry and thirsty; we are clothed in rags; we are beaten; we wander from place to place . . .

Thought: 'We are weak and despised - you are strong and honoured.'

Prayer: Lord, we pray today for those Christians who are hungry, thirsty, exhausted, ill-treated or homeless. May we who are strong, healthy, well-clothed and fed, do something to help and encourage them. Amen.

Day 7

1 Corinthians 4.12-14
. . . we wear ourselves out with hard work. When we are cursed, we bless; when we are persecuted, we endure; when we are insulted, we answer with kind words. We are no more than this world's refuse; we are the scum of the earth to this very moment! I write this . . . not because I want to make you feel ashamed, but to instruct you as my own dear children.

Thought: It is 'hard work' to give blessing for cursing and kind words for insults!

Prayer: Lord, please help us to make a real effort to be loving to people who are unloving to us, and to return kind words for harsh ones. Amen.

Week 28

Day 1

1 Corinthians 10.12-13

Whoever thinks he is standing firm had better be careful that he does not fall. Every test that you have experienced is the kind that normally comes to people. But God keeps his promise, and he will not allow you to be tested beyond your power to remain firm; at the time you are put to the test, he will give you the strength to endure it, and so provide you with a way out.

Thought: What is your particular 'test'?

Prayer: Father, You know that our particular temptation is . . . but You have promised that You will give us the strength to remain firm, and provide us with a way out. Please remind us of this next time we are tested. Amen.

Day 2

1 Corinthians 10.23-4

'We are allowed to do anything,' so they say. That is true, but not everything is good. 'We are allowed to do anything' - but not everything is helpful. No one should be looking to his own interests, but to the interests of others.

Thought: 'I can do what I like!' - True or false?

Prayer: May all that I do and say help others to see,
That Jesus is my Lord, and He lives in me.
Amen.

Day 3

1 Corinthians 10.29-31

'Well, then,' someone asks, 'why should my freedom to act be limited by another person's conscience? If I thank God for my food, why should anyone criticize me about food for which I give thanks?'

Well, whatever you do, whether you eat or drink, do it all for God's glory.

Thought: 'Do it all for Christ's glory!'

Prayer: Lord, remind us that our daily aim should be to do everything for Your glory. Amen.

Day 4

1 Corinthians 10.32-3
Live in such a way as to cause no trouble either to Jews or Gentiles or to the church of God. Just do as I do; I try to please everyone in all that I do, not thinking of my own good, but of the good of all, so that they might be saved.

Thought: "Not thinking of my own good, but of the good of all."

Prayer: Lord Jesus, help us to remember that we are members of a family: our own human family and the family of Your church. Teach us to consider the good of all, and not just our own personal wishes and concerns. Amen.

Day 5

1 Corinthians 12.4-6
There are different kinds of spiritual gifts, but the same Spirit gives them. There are different ways of serving, but the same Lord is served. There are different abilities to perform service, but the same God gives ability to everyone for their particular service.

Thought: What is your gift?

Prayer: Show us today, Lord, what our particular gifts are, and help us to use them in our home and in our church, for the benefit of others. Amen.

Day 6

1 Corinthians 12.14-16
For the body itself is not made up of only one part, but of many parts. If the foot were to say, 'Because I am not a hand, I don't belong to the body,' that would not keep it from being a part of the body. And if the ear were to say, 'Because I am not an eye, I don't belong to the body,' that would not keep it from being a part of the body.

Thought: Unattached hands and feet are useless.

Prayer: Father, teach us that we belong to Your body, the Church, and that only by working together in harmony can we be fully used by You. Amen.

Day 7

1 Corinthians 12.17-20
If the whole body were just an eye, how could it hear? And if it were only an ear, how could it smell? As it is, however, God put every different part

in the body just as He wanted it to be. There would not be a body if it were all only one part! As it is, there are many parts but one body.

Thought: 'Many parts but one body . . . '

Prayer: Lord, ears are for listening, eyes are for seeing, lips are for speaking, hands are for helping, feet are for going; show us if You want us to be ears, or eyes, or lips, or hands or feet in the body of Your church. Amen.

Week 29

Today we begin the Old Testament story of Abram, a man who loved God and was prepared to obey Him, whatever the cost. Later God changed his name to Abraham - a name which meant 'father of many nations.'

Day 1

Genesis 12.1-2

The Lord said to Abram, 'Leave your native land, your relatives, and your father's home, and go to a country that I am going to show you. I will give you many descendants, and they will become a great nation. I will bless you and make your name famous, so that you will be a blessing.'

Thought: Obedience to God sometimes means moving!

Prayer: Dear Father God, when You speak, may we listen, and when You bring change into our lives, help us to be prepared to accept it. Amen.

Day 2

Genesis 13.1, 5-7

Abram went north out of Egypt to the southern part of Canaan with his wife and everything he owned, and Lot went with him.

    Lot also had sheep, goats, and cattle, as well as his own family and servants. And so there was not enough pasture land for the two of them to stay together, because they had too many animals. So quarrels broke out between the men who took care of Abram's animals, and those who took care of Lot's animals.

Thought: Riches do not necessarily bring contentment.

Prayer: Lord Jesus Christ, You taught us that true happiness is not found in owning material things. Give us, and those we love, the contentment that is only found in You. Amen.

Day 3

Genesis 13.8-9

Then Abram said to Lot, 'We are relatives, and your men and my men shouldn't be quarrelling. So let's separate. Choose any part of the land you want. You go one way, and I'll go the other.'

Thought: Are we peacemakers?

Prayer: Lord, show us how to live at peace with each other, forgoing our own rights and seeking the good of others. Amen.

Day 4

Genesis 13.10-13

Lot looked round and saw that the whole Jordan Valley, all the way to Zoar, had plenty of water, like the Garden of the Lord or like the land of Egypt. (This was before the Lord had destroyed the cities of Sodom and Gomorrah.) So Lot chose the whole Jordan Valley for himself and moved away towards the east. That is how the two men parted. Abram stayed in the land of Canaan, and Lot settled among the cities in the valley and camped near Sodom, whose people were wicked and sinned against the Lord.

Thought: Temptation often accompanies material prosperity!

Prayer: Dear Father God, give us wisdom to make the right choices, and grant that the desire for material gain may not lead us into temptation. Amen.

Day 5

Genesis 13.14-18

After Lot had left, the Lord said to Abram, 'From where you are, look carefully in all directions. I am going to give you and your descendants all the land that you see, and it will be yours for ever. I am going to give you so many descendants that no one will be able to count them all; it would be as easy to count all the specks of dust on earth! Now go and look over the whole land, because I am going to give it all to you.'

So Abram moved his camp and settled near the sacred trees of Mamre at Hebron, and there he built an altar to the Lord.

Thought: 'From where you are, look carefully in all directions . . . '

Prayer: Lord God, we are here in . . . May we take time to look carefully in all directions . . . (at our home, our schools, our church, our job, our friends . . .) and see if the time has come to make changes, or if we are in the place where You want us to be. Amen.

Day 6

Genesis 15.1-2, 5; 21.1, 2

After this, Abram had a vision and heard the Lord say to him, 'Do not be afraid, Abram. I will shield you from danger and give you a great reward.'

But Abram answered, 'Sovereign Lord, what good will your reward do me, since I have no children?' . . . The Lord took him outside and said, 'Look at the sky and try to count the stars; you will have as many descendants as that.'

. . . The Lord blessed Sarah, as he had promised, and she became pregnant and bore a son to Abraham when he was old.'

Thought: To God all things are possible.

Prayer: Lord, You know that there are times when we find it hard to remember that You are all-powerful and Almighty and we limit Your authority and potential to human understanding. Forgive us and give us renewed confidence in Your greatness. Amen.

Note: The child born to Sarah and Abraham was a little boy, whom they named Isaac. Although Abraham loved his son dearly, he always put God first throughout his long life. When Isaac was old enough to marry, Abraham wanted to be sure that Isaac's wife was a believing Jew, so he sent a trusted servant back to Mesopotamia, where he knew some of his relatives were still living, on a very important mission!

Day 7

Genesis 24.1-4

Abraham was now very old, and the Lord had blessed him in everything he did. He said to his oldest servant, who was in charge of all that he had, 'Place your hand between my thighs and make a vow. I want you to make a vow in the name of the Lord, the God of heaven and earth, that you will not choose a wife for my son from the people here in Canaan. You must go back to the country where I was born and get a wife for my son Isaac from among my relatives.'

Thought: A married couple need to have the same Lord.

Prayer: Lord, we pray today for young people who are considering marriage (especially . . .). Help them to make a wise decision and to choose someone who shares their faith. Amen.

Week 30

Day 1

Genesis 24.10-12

The servant, who was in charge of Abraham's property, took ten of his master's camels and went to the city where Nahor had lived in northern Mesopotamia. When he arrived, he made the camels kneel down at the well outside the city. It was late afternoon, the time when women came out to get water. He prayed, 'Lord, God of my master Abraham, give me success today and keep your promise to my master.'

Thought: Prayer is the key to success.

Prayer: Teach us, Heavenly Father, to pray before we act, so that whatever we do may be in accordance with Your will. Amen.

Day 2

Genesis 24.15-18

Before he had finished praying, Rebecca arrived with a water-jar on her shoulder. She was the daughter of Bethuel, who was the son of Abraham's brother Nahor and his wife Milcah. She was a very beautiful young girl and still a virgin. She went down to the well, filled her jar, and came back. The servant ran to meet her and said, 'Please give me a drink of water from your jar.'

Thought: People judge us by our actions.

Prayer: Lord, make us kind in word and deed,
Helping others in their need.   Amen.

Day 3

Genesis 24.19-21

When he had finished, she said, 'I will also bring water for your camels and let them have all they want.' She quickly emptied her jar into the animals' drinking-trough and ran to the well to get more water, until she had watered all his camels. The man kept watching her in silence, to see if the Lord had given him success.

Thought: Do we do *more* than we are asked to do?

Prayer: Father in Heaven, give us seeing eyes to recognise the needs of others, and willing hands and feet with which to meet those needs. Amen.

Day 4

Genesis 24.23-7

He said, 'Please tell me who your father is. Is there room in his house for my men and me to spend the night?'

'My father is Bethuel son of Nahor and Milcah,' she answered. 'There is plenty of straw and fodder at our house, and there is a place for you to stay.'

Then the man knelt down and worshipped the Lord. He said, 'Praise the Lord, the God of my master Abraham, who has faithfully kept his promise to my master. The Lord has led me straight to my master's relatives.'

Thought: 'At our house . . . there is a place for you to stay . . . '

Prayer: Dear Father God, help us to warmly welcome in our home all who need a place to stay. Amen.

Day 5

Genesis 24.32-3

So the man went into the house, and Laban unloaded the camels and gave them straw and fodder. Then he brought water for Abraham's servant and his men to wash their feet. When food was brought, the man said, 'I will not eat until I have said what I have to say.'

Thought: Which comes first - our duty or our comfort?

Prayer: Dear Father God, help us to put our duty before the satisfaction of our bodily needs when we have something important to do for You. Amen.

Day 6

Genesis 24.42-4

'When I came to the well today, I prayed, "Lord, God of my master Abraham, please give me success in what I am doing. Here I am at the well. When a young woman comes out to get water, I will ask her to give me a drink of water from her jar. If she agrees and also offers to bring water for my camels, may she be the one that you have chosen as the wife for my master's son."'

Thought: What did the servant's 'test' show about Rebecca?

Prayer: Lord, we know our actions show the kind of people we are; please help us to be kind, willing, and thoughtful. Amen.

Day 7

Genesis 24.45-6

'Before I had finished my silent prayer, Rebecca came with a water-jar on her shoulder and went down to the well to get water. I said to her, "Please give me a drink." She quickly lowered her jar from her shoulder and said, "Drink, and I will also water your camels." So I drank, and she watered the camels.'

Thought: Answers to prayer sometimes come more quickly than we expect!

Prayer: Father God, thank You for answered prayer (especially . . .), but please help us to go on praying when we do not see our prayers answered immediately and we wonder if they are going to be answered at all. Amen.

Week 31

Day 1

Genesis 24.50-2

Laban and Bethuel answered, 'Since this matter comes from the Lord, it is not for us to make a decision. Here is Rebecca; take her and go. Let her become the wife of your master's son, as the Lord himself has said.' When the servant of Abraham heard this, he bowed down and worshipped the Lord.

Thought: Do we obey promptly when we believe a 'matter comes from the Lord'?

Prayer: God our Father, help us to recognise Your plans and make us prompt in carrying them through. Amen.

Day 2

Genesis 24.55-6

But Rebecca's brother and her mother said, 'Let the girl stay with us a week or ten days, and then she may go.'

But he said, 'Don't make us stay. The Lord has made my journey a success; let me go back to my master.'

Thought: Never put off until tomorrow what should be done today!

Prayer: Lord Jesus, please forgive us when we put off until a more convenient time things that should be done promptly, and bring to our minds anything of importance that we have left undone. Amen.

Day 3

Genesis 24.57

They answered, 'Let's call the girl and find out what she has to say.' So they called Rebecca and asked, 'Do you want to go with this man?'

'Yes,' she answered.

Thought: Rebecca did not waste words!

Prayer: Father God, sometimes we waste time and words in useless arguments and discussions when a straight answer is all that is needed. Please forgive us. Amen.

Day 4

Genesis 24.59-61

So they let Rebecca and her old family servant go with Abraham's servant and his men. And they gave Rebecca their blessing in these words:

'May you, sister, become the mother of millions!

May your descendants conquer the cities of their enemies!'

Then Rebecca and her young women got ready and mounted the camels to go with Abraham's servant, and they all started out.

Thought: 'They gave Rebecca their blessing . . . and they all started out.'

Prayer: Lord, please be with those who journey today (especially . . .). Watch over them and keep them safe, we pray. Amen.

Day 5

Genesis 24.62-3

Isaac had come into the wilderness of "The Well of the Living One Who Sees Me" and was staying in the southern part of Canaan. He went out in the early evening to take a walk in the fields and saw camels coming.

Thought: A quiet walk gives time for thought.

Prayer: Father God, when we face great changes in our lives, remind us to prepare ourselves by finding the time to be quiet in Your presence. Amen.

Day 6

Genesis 24.66-7

The servant told Isaac everything he had done. Then Isaac brought Rebecca into the tent that his mother Sarah had lived in, and she became his wife. Isaac loved Rebecca, and so he was comforted for the loss of his mother.

Thought: Are you used to comfort the bereaved?

Prayer: Lord, please be with those who are bereaved (especially . . .) and show us how we can best bring comfort to them. Amen.

Day 7

Genesis 25.7-8, 11

Abraham died at the ripe old age of a hundred and seventy five. After the death of Abraham, God blessed his son Isaac, who lived near "The Well of the Living One Whe Sees Me."

Thought: God's blessing is on everyone who draws livng water from "The Well of the Living One."

Prayer: Lord, we remember with love and thankfulness all your servants who remained faithful to You throughout their lives - (especially . . .). May we, in our turn, be blessed by You, as we try to follow their example. Amen.

Week 32

We are going to look at some verses from the book of Joshua this week.
Joshua took over the leadership of the Israelite people from Moses;
it was in God's plans to give his people a new life in the land of Canaan -
but the invasion resulted in a lot of suffering on both sides.

Day 1

Joshua 1.1-2

After the death of the Lord's servant Moses, the Lord spoke to Moses'
helper, Joshua son of Nun. He said, 'My servant Moses is dead. Get ready
now, you and all the people of Israel, and cross the River Jordan into the
land that I am giving them.'

Thought: We should make sure that leaders have 'understudies'.

Prayer: Heavenly Father, remind us that Your work must go on, even if
our present leaders die, or are set aside. Help us to train others to take their
place. Amen.

Day 2

Joshua 1.5

'Joshua, no one will be able to defeat you as long as you live. I will be with
you as I was with Moses. I will always be with you; I will never abandon
you.'

Thought: 'I will always be with you . . . '

Prayer: Almighty God, sometimes the job that You are asking us to do
seems too big or hard for us. Remind us that nothing is too big or too hard
if You are with us. Amen.

Day 3

Joshua 1.6-7

'Be determined and confident, for you will be the leader of these people
as they occupy this land which I promised their ancestors. Just be determined, be confident; and make sure that you obey the whole Law that my
servant Moses gave you. Do not neglect any part of it and you will succeed
wherever you go.'

Thought: 'Be determined, be confident . . . obey the whole Law . . . '

Prayer: Lord, Your commandments are still important for us today. Help us as individuals, as a family, as a Church, and as a nation, to live by them, with determination and confidence. Amen.

Day 4

Joshua 1.8-9

'Be sure that the book of the Law is always read in your worship. Study it day and night, and make sure that you obey everything written in it. Then you will be prosperous and successful. Remember that I have commanded you to be determined and confident! Don't be afraid or discouraged, for I, the Lord your God, am with you wherever you go.'

Thought: What is God's 'recipe' for prosperity and success?

Prayer: Lord, help us to be aware of the importance of reading and studying Your Word, but, most of all, give us wisdom and courage to obey its teaching. Amen.

Day 5

Joshua 1.10-11

Then Joshua ordered the leaders to go through the camp and say to the people, 'Get some food ready, because in three days you are going to cross the River Jordan to occupy the land that the Lord your God is giving you.'

Thought: Leaders need to be aware of practical as well as spiritual issues.

Prayer: Lord, when we are in positions of leadership help us to be aware of both the bodily and spiritual needs of the people for whom we are responsible. Amen.

Day 6

Joshua 1.16-17

They answered Joshua, 'We will do everything you have told us and will go wherever you send us. We will obey you, just as we always obeyed Moses, and may the Lord your God be with you as he was with Moses!'

Thought: Do we give parents, teachers, employers, Church Ministers, or even God, this kind of complete obedience?

Prayer: Lord, we pray today for those who are set in authority over us (especially . . .). Help us to be obedient to them, remembering to pray that You will make them wise in their positions of authority, and in the decisions that must be made. Amen.

Day 7

Joshua 3.1, 5

The next morning Joshua and all the people of Israel got up early, left the camp at Acacia, and went to the Jordan, where they camped while waiting to cross it . . .

Joshua said to the people, 'Purify yourselves, because tomorrow the Lord will perform miracles among you.'

Thought: Purification precedes miracles.

Prayer: Heavenly Father, You know we sometimes long to see miraculous things happening in our Church and in the lives of Your people. Remind us that You cannot use us unless we are spiritually clean and obedient. Amen.

Note: The invasion of Canaan is a long and exciting story. Joshua proved to be an inspiring leader and was faithful to God right up to the day of his death at one hundred and ten! You may like to read the rest of story for yourself.

Week 33

Gideon considered himself to be weak and unimportant, but because of his faith and trust in God, he became one of Israel's national heroes! This is the story of how God enabled Gideon to defeat the huge army of Midian with only 300 men.

Day 1

Judges 6.11-13

Then the Lord's angel came to the village of Ophrah and sat under the oak-tree that belonged to Joash, a man of the clan of Abiezer. His son Gideon was threshing some wheat secretly in a winepress, so that the Midianites would not see him. The Lord's angel appeared to him there and said, 'The Lord is with you, brave and mighty man!'

Gideon said to him, 'If I may ask, sir, why has all this happened to us if the Lord is with us? What about the wonderful things that our fathers told us the Lord used to do - how he brought them out of Egypt? The Lord has abandoned us and left us to the mercy of the Midianites.'

Thought: Are you honest with God about the way you feel?

Prayer: Lord, we know we cannot hide anything from You; so teach us to be completely honest with You about what we think and feel. Amen.

Day 2

Judges 6.14-16

Then the Lord ordered him, 'Go with all your great strength and rescue Israel from the Midianites. I myself am sending you.'

Gideon replied, 'But how can I rescue Israel? My clan is the weakest in the tribe of Manesseh, and I am the least important member of my family'

The Lord answered, 'You can do it because I will help you. You will crush the Midianites as easily as if they were only one man.'

Thought: God sees what we *can* be as well as what we *are*!

Prayer: Please God, help us to become strong and brave in Your service, even though we sometimes feel weak and cowardly. Amen.

Day 3

Judges 7.2-3

The Lord said to Gideon, 'The men you have are too many for me to give them victory over the Midianites. They might think that they had won by themselves, and so give me no credit. Announce to the people, "Anyone who is afraid should go back home, and we will stay here at Mount Gilead."' So twenty-two thousand went back, but ten thousand stayed.

Thought: Would you have been among the twenty-two thousand or the ten thousand?

Prayer: Lord, You know we are sometimes afraid, even though we do not want to admit it (especially of . . .). Give us the courage to follow You wherever You may lead, trusting in Your strength and not our own. Amen.

Day 4

Judges 7.4, 5-6

Then the Lord said to Gideon, 'You still have too many men. Take them down to the water, and I will separate them for you there . . . ' Gideon took the men down to the water, and the Lord said to him, 'Separate everyone who laps up the water with his tongue like a dog, from everyone who gets down on his knees to drink.' There were three hundred men who scooped up water in their hands and lapped it; all the others got down on their knees to drink.

Thought: Sometimes we have to trust God's selection procedures even when we do not fully understand them.

Prayer: Lord, help us to be watchful for attacks from the enemy, who can attack us when we least expect it. Amen.

Day 5

Judges 7.7-8

The Lord said to Gideon, 'I will rescue you and give you victory over the Midianites with the three hundred men who lapped the water. Tell everyone else to go home.' So Gideon sent all the Israelites home, except the three hundred, who kept all the supplies and trumpets. The Midianite camp was below them in the valley.

Thought: Small in number but great in faith.

Prayer: Lord, we pray today for small groups of Christians who are living

and working for You in different parts of the world (especially . . .).
Encourage them, and fill them with Your Holy Spirit of power and
strength. Amen.

Day 6

Judges 7.16-18
He [Gideon] divided his three hundred men into three groups and gave
each man a trumpet and a jar with a torch inside it. He told them, 'When
I get to the edge of the camp, watch me, and do what I do. When my group
and I blow our trumpets, then you blow yours all round the camp and
shout, "For the Lord and for Gideon!"'

Thought: Would we dare say, 'Watch me and do what I do'?

Prayer: Lord Jesus, You are our only pattern and example. May we watch
You and do what You would do, each day of our lives. Amen.

Day 7

Judges 7.19-21
Gideon and his hundred men came to the edge of the camp a short while
before midnight, just after the guard had been changed. Then they blew
the trumpets and broke the jars they were holding, and the other two
groups did the same. They all held the torches in their left hands, the
trumpets in their right, and shouted, 'A sword for the Lord and for
Gideon!' Every man stood in his place round the camp, and the whole
enemy army ran away yelling.

Thought: Obedience results in victory.

Prayer: Loving Father God, please teach us to obey every whisper of Your
voice, so that we may gain the victory over sin, selfishness, and temptation. Amen.

Week 34

*For the next three weeks we are going to look at the first part of a
letter St Paul wrote to the church at Thessalonica, (the capital city of
the Roman province of Macedonia) encouraging them to go on working
quietly while waiting, in hope, for the return of the Lord Jesus Christ - a
return for which we still wait today.*

Day 1

1 Thessalonians 1.1, 2
From Paul, Silas, and Timothy -
To the people of the church in Thessalonica, who belong to God the
Father and the Lord Jesus Christ:
May grace and peace be yours.
We always thank God for you all and always mention you in our
prayers.

Thought: Do you pray for your Church?

Prayer: Dear God, we pray today for the people of our Church of . . . who
belong to God the Father, and the Lord Jesus Christ.
May grace and peace be with them. Amen.

Day 2

1 Thessalonians 1.3
For we remember before our God and Father how you put your faith into
practice, how your love made you work so hard, and how your hope in
our Lord Jesus Christ is firm.

Thought: 'Faith, love, hope and hard work . . . '

Prayer: Lord, help us to put our faith into practice; give us love which
shows itself in action, and a firm hope in You. Amen.

Day 3

1 Thessalonians 1.4, 5
Our brothers, we know that God loves you and has chosen you to be his
own. For we brought the Good News to you, not with words only, but also
with power and the Holy Spirit, and with complete conviction of its truth.
You know how we lived when we were with you; it was for your own
good.

Thought: 'You did not choose me; I chose you and appointed you to go and bear much fruit, the kind of fruit that endures.'   (John 15.16)

Prayer: Thank You, Lord Jesus, for loving and choosing us to be Your own. Fill us with Your Holy Spirit, so that we may live and work for Your glory. Amen.

Day 4

1 Thessalonians 1.6-7
You imitated us and the Lord; and even though you suffered much, you received the message with the joy that comes from the Holy Spirit. So you became an example to all believers in Macedonia and Achaia.

Thought: 'There is nothing the body suffers the soul may not profit by.'
George Meredith (1828-1909)

Prayer: Dear Father God, we know that life brings to all of us sadness and suffering, as well as happiness and joy (we think particularly of . . . today). Thank You for those who are an inspiration to us because of their courage, hope and joy. Amen.

Day 5

1 Thessalonians 1.8
For not only did the message about the Lord go out from you throughout Macedonia and Achaia, but the news about your faith in God has gone everywhere. There is nothing, then, that we need to say.

Thought: 'Words are also actions, and actions are a kind of words.'
Ralph Waldo Emerson (1803-1882)

Prayer: Heavenly Father, we know that people watch us, to see if the way we behave matches up to our Christian profession. Help us to hold on to our faith and to pass it on to others. Amen.

Day 6

1 Thessalonians 1.9-10
All those people speak about how you received us when we visited you, and how you turned away from idols to God, to serve the true and living God and to wait for his Son to come from heaven - his Son Jesus, whom he raised from death and who rescues us from God's anger that is coming.

Thought: 'I am going to prepare a place for you . . . I will come back.'
(John 14.2, 3)

Prayer: Lord, today we remember Your promise to us that you are coming back. We have been a long time waiting for You, but please remind us that You keep Your promises, and grant that, when You do come, You will find us living and working in the way You want us to. Amen.

Day 7

1 Thessalonians 2.1-2

Our brothers, you yourselves know that our visit to you was not a failure. You know how we had already been ill-treated and insulted in Philippi before we came to you in Thessalonica. And even though there was much opposition, our God gave us courage to tell you the Good News that comes from him.

Thought: Courage in opposition!

Prayer: Dear Father God, we pray today for those who are being ill-treated and insulted because of their faith in You (especially . . .). Give them the faith to hold on to what they believe against all opposition. Amen.

Week 35

Day 1

1 Thessalonians 2.3-4
Our appeal to you is not based on error or impure motives, nor do we try to trick anyone. Instead, we always speak as God wants us to, because he has judged us worthy to be entrusted with the Good News. We do not try to please men, but to please God, who tests our motives.

Thought: Do we try to please men or please God?

Prayer: Lord, You know we are often more anxious to please men, than to please You. Help us to speak and act as You want us to. Amen.

Day 2

1 Thessalonians 2.5-7
You know very well that we did not come to you with flattering talk, nor did we use words to cover up greed - God is our witness! We did not try to get praise from anyone, either from you or from others, even though as apostles of Christ we could have made demands on you. But we were gentle when we were with you, like a mother taking care of her children.

Thought: Gentle, like a mother taking care of her children . . .
          'The gentle mind by gentle deeds is known.'
                                        Edmund Spenser (1552-99)

Prayer: Heavenly Father, You deal gently with us, but we confess we often fail to deal gently with others - even members of our own family, or of our own Church. Forgive us, and teach us to be gentle with each other. Amen.

Day 3

1 Thessalonians 2.8
Because of our love for you we were ready to share with you not only the Good News from God but even our own lives. You were so dear to us!

Thought: Sharing our lives *is* costly!

Prayer: Lord, help us to share with others our money, our time, our home, our talents, and our very lives, however costly it may prove. Amen.

Day 4

1 Thessalonians 2.9

Surely you remember, our brothers, how we worked and toiled! We worked day and night so that we would not be any trouble to you as we preached to you the Good News from God.

Thought: There are no 'fixed hours' for those whose work is preaching the gospel.

Prayer: Almighty God, we are sometimes ashamed when we realise how little of our time and energy is spent in worship and Christian work, when there are those who work and toil, day and night, in order to preach Your gospel. Forgive us, and help us to review the way we spend our time and talents. Amen.

Day 5

1 Thessalonians 2.10-12

You are our witnesses, and so is God, that our conduct towards you who believe was pure, right, and without fault. You know that we treated each one of you just as a father treats his own children. We encouraged you, we comforted you, and we kept urging you to live the kind of life that pleases God, who calls you to share in his own Kingdom and glory.

Thought: 'Encourage, comfort, and urge . . . '

Prayer: Lord, there are people we know who need encouragement (especially . . .); there are people we know who need comfort (especially . . .); and there are people we know who need urging if they are to live the kind of lives that please You, and share in Your kingdom and glory (especially . . .). Help us to recognise different people's needs, and to meet them, in Your strength. Amen.

Day 6

1 Thessalonians 4.11-12

Make it your aim to live a quiet life, to mind your own business, and to earn your own living, just as we told you before. In this way you will win the respect of those who are not believers, and you will not have to depend on anyone for what you need.

Thought: The secret of how we can gain respect from non-believers is found in verse 11!

Prayer: Thank You, dear Father, that we can depend on You for everything we need. Help us to gain the respect of those who are not believers (especially . . .) so that, in Your good time, we may be able to witness to them about You. Amen.

Day 7

1 Thessalonians 4.13-14
Our brothers, we want you to know the truth about those who have died, so that you will not be sad, as are those who have no hope. We believe that Jesus died and rose again, and so we believe that God will take back with Jesus those who have died believing in him.

Thought: ' . . . you will not be sad, as are those who have no hope . . . '

Prayer: Lord Jesus, thank You for proving by Your resurrection, that death is only a door to eternal life. We pray today for those who mourn (particularly . . .); please strengthen their faith and hope, and give us the right words of reassurance to comfort them. Amen.

Week 36

Day 1

1 Thessalonians 4.16, 17-18

Those who have died believing in Christ will rise to life first; then we who are living at that time will be gathered up along with them in the clouds to meet the Lord in the air. And so we will always be with the Lord. So then, encourage one another with these words.

Thought: 'Encourage one another with these words.'

Prayer: Almighty God, help us to encourage one another with the sure hope that one day we will all be together with You, and You will 'wipe away all tears from our eyes, there will be no more death, no more grief or crying or pain, for the old things will have disappeared,'* and You will live with us, and we shall be Your people. For ever and ever. Amen.
*[Revelation 21.1-4]

Day 2

1 Thessalonians 5.2, 4

For you yourselves know very well that the Day of the Lord will come as a thief comes at night . . . But you, brothers, are not in the darkness, and the Day should not take you by surprise like a thief.

Thought: Are you likely to be taken 'by surprise' when the Lord comes again?

Prayer: Lord Jesus, we often forget that You have promised to come again to the earth; help us to be ready and waiting. Amen.

Day 3

1 Thessalonians 5.5-8

All of you are people who belong to the light, who belong to the day. We do not belong to the night or to the darkness. So then, we should not be sleeping like the others; we should be awake and sober. It is at night that people sleep; it is at night that they get drunk. But we belong to the day, and we should be sober.

Thought: Are we happy for all our words and actions to be open to the light?

Prayer: Lord, we confess that there are certain parts of our lives of which we are ashamed and would not like to be open to the light. Forgive us, and help us to live like people of the light, who belong to the day, so that there is nothing we need to hide from You, or from other people. Amen.

Day 4

1 Thessalonians 5.8-10
We must wear faith and love as a breastplate, and our hope of salvation as a helmet. God did not choose us to suffer his anger, but to possess salvation through our Lord Jesus Christ, who died for us in order that we might live together with him, whether we are alive or dead when he comes.

Thought: What is a Christian's 'breastplate' and 'helmet' and what part of the body do they protect?

Prayer: Heavenly Father, fill us with faith, hope, and love! Thank you for choosing us to possess salvation, through Your Son, our Lord Jesus Christ. Amen.

Day 5

1 Thessalonians 5.12-13
We beg you, our brothers, to pay proper respect to those who work among you, who guide and instruct you in the Christian life. Treat them with the greatest respect and love because of the work they do. Be at peace among yourselves.

Thought: Do you treat your minister with respect and love?

Prayers: Dear Father God, we confess we do not often pray for . . . who works among us trying to guide and instruct people in the Christian life. Show us some practical way in which we can assure them that we respect and love them. Amen.

Day 6

1 Thessalonians 5.14-15
We urge you, our brothers, to warn the idle, encourage the timid, help the weak, be patient with everyone. See that no one pays back wrong for wrong, but at all times make it your aim to do good to one another and to all people.

Thought: '. . . be patient with everyone . . . '

Prayer: Dear Lord, we find it so hard to be patient with idle, timid and weak people (especially . . .), and yet we know they are the very ones who need our love, understanding, and encouragement. Give us Your patience as we make it our aim to do good to one another and to all people. Amen.

Day 7

1 Thessalonians 5.16-22
Be joyful always, pray at all times, be thankful in all circumstances. This is what God wants from you in your life, in union with Christ Jesus.

Do not restrain the Holy Spirit; do not despise inspired messages. Put all things to the test: keep what is good and avoid every kind of evil.

Thought: More things are wrought by prayer than this world dreams of.
Alfred, Lord Tennyson (1809-92)

Prayer: Lord Jesus, help us to be joyful, to pray and to be thankful, and to put all things to the test; to keep what is good and avoid every kind of evil. For Your Name's sake. Amen.

Week 37

The book of Job is about a good man who lost all his children and his property, and become ill with a horrible disease. He could not understand why God had let all these bad things happen to him, but he still trusted God.

Day 1

Job 1.1-3

There was a man named Job, living in the land of Uz, who worshipped God and was faithful to him. He was a good man, careful not to do anything evil. He had seven sons and three daughters, and owned seven thousand sheep, three thousand camels, one thousand head of cattle, and five hundred donkeys. He also had a large number of servants and was the richest man in the East.

Thought: Verse 1 is more important than verses 2 and 3.

Prayer: Dear God, please help us to worship You, and be faithful to You, and make us careful not to do anything that is wrong. Amen.

Day 2

Job 1.4-5

Job's sons used to take it in turns to give a feast, to which all the others would come, and they always invited their three sisters to join them. The morning after each feast, Job would get up early and offer sacrifices for each of his children in order to purify them. He always did this because he thought that one of them might have sinned by insulting God unintentionally.

Thought: Do you get up early to pray, after a late night party?

Prayer: Lord, remind us to care for the spiritual health of members of our own family. We think especially today of . . . Watch over them and bless them we pray. Amen.

Day 3

Job 1.6-8

When the day came for the heavenly beings to appear before the Lord, Satan was there among them. The Lord asked him, 'What have you been doing?'

Satan answered, 'I have been walking here and there, roaming round the earth.'

'Did you notice my servant Job?' the Lord asked. 'There is no one on earth as faithful and good as he is. He worships me and is careful not to do anything evil.'

Thought: Put your own name, instead of 'Job' in verse 8. Does the rest of the verse describe you?

Prayer: Father, we confess that we often fail to please You by the way we live; forgive us and help us to serve You better. Amen.

Day 4

Job 1.9-12

Satan replied, 'Would Job worship you if he got nothing out of it? You have always protected him and his family and everything he owns. You bless everything he does, and you have given him enough cattle to fill the whole country. But now suppose you take away everything he has - he will curse you to your face!'

'All right,' the Lord said to Satan, 'everything he has is in your power, but you must not hurt Job himself.' So Satan left.

Thought: It is easy to be a Christian when things go well.

Prayer: Dear Lord, thank You for the way You have blessed and protected us; when troubles and difficulties come into our lives, please help us to continue to trust in You. Amen.

Day 5

Job 1.13-16

One day when Job's children were having a feast at the home of their eldest brother, a messenger came running to Job. 'We were ploughing the fields with the oxen,' he said, 'and the donkeys were in a nearby pasture. Suddenly the Sabeans attacked and stole them all. They killed every one of your servants except me. I am the only one who escaped to tell you.'

Before he had finished speaking, another servant came and said, 'Lightning struck the sheep and the shepherds and killed them all. I am the only one who escaped to tell you.'

Thought: How important to you are your possessions?

Prayer: Please God, help us to hold the things of this world lightly, so that however great are our material losses, we may still hold fast to our faith in You. Amen.

Day 6

Job 1.17-19

Before he had finished speaking, another servant came and said, 'Three bands of Chaldean raiders attacked us, took away the camels, and killed all your servants except me. I am the only one who escaped to tell you.'

Before he had finished speaking, another servant came and said, 'Your children were having a feast at the home of your eldest son, when a storm swept in from the desert. It blew the house down and killed them all. I am the only one who escaped to tell you.'

Thought: Jesus did not promise that being a Christian would protect His followers from all disasters.

Prayer: Father, we pray for all those who are mourning the loss of a loved one today, and thinking especially of those killed or injured in natural disasters. Give them Your comfort, strength and peace. Amen.

Day 7

Job 1.20-2

Then Job stood up and tore his clothes in grief. He shaved his head and threw himself face downwards on the ground. He said, 'I was born with nothing, and I will die with nothing. The Lord gave, and now he has taken away. May his name be praised!'

In spite of everything that had happened, Job did not sin by blaming God.

Thought: Are you able to say 'His name be praised!' when bad things happen to you, as well as when good things happen?

Prayer: Lord Jesus, we find it easy to say 'Praise the Lord!' when good things happen, but we thank You for all your servants who stand firm under great trials, sorrows and difficulties. Help us to be more like them, we pray You. Amen.

Note: I am sure you will be pleased to know that the story of Job ended happily! You may like to turn to Job 42 verses 7-16 and read about it. God blessed the last part of Job's life even more than he had blessed the first, and he died at a very great age, long enough to see his grandchildren and great grandchildren!

Week 38

You will remember reading about Abraham's servant choosing a wife for Isaac, who was named Rebecca. In time Rebecca had twin boys called Jacob and Esau. Rebecca favoured Jacob but Isaac favoured Esau. We are going to read about a time when this family favouritism led to a lot of trouble!

Day 1

Genesis 25.27-8

The boys grew up, and Esau became a skilled hunter, a man who loved the outdoor life, but Jacob was a quiet man who stayed at home. Isaac preferred Esau, because he enjoyed eating the animals Esau killed, but Rebecca preferred Jacob.

Thought: It is unwise to have 'favourites' within a family!

Prayer: Lord Jesus, give each member of our family an equal love for the other, and give all of us an overruling love for You. Amen.

Day 2

Genesis 25.29-30

One day while Jacob was cooking some bean soup, Esau came in from hunting. He was hungry and said to Jacob, 'I'm starving; give me some of that red stuff.'

Thought: 'He was hungry and said . . . "I'm starving . . ."'

Prayer: Dear Father God, may those of us who have a healthy appetite, and the means to satisfy it, remember those who are truly starving; and motivate us to help them. Amen.

Day 3

Genesis 25.31-32

Jacob answered, 'I will give it to you if you give me your rights as the first-born son.'

Esau said, 'All right! I am about to die; what good will my rights do me then?'

Thought: 'I will give it to you if you give me . . .'

Prayer: Lord, teach us to take a joy in giving without looking for anything in return; for Your dear sake. Amen.

Day 4

Genesis 25.33-4

Jacob answered, 'First make a vow that you will give me your rights.' Esau made the vow and gave his rights to Jacob. Then Jacob gave him some bread and some of the soup. He ate and drank and then got up and left. That was all Esau cared about his rights as the first-born son.

Thought: Esau did not value his 'rights' - do we?

Prayer: Almighty God, thank You for the privileges that we enjoy; peace, education, free-speech, health care, and many more. Help us to value and appreciate them and to remember those who are less fortunate than we are (especially . . .). Amen.

Day 5

Genesis 27.1-4

Isaac was now old and had become blind. He sent for his elder son Esau and said to him, 'My son!'

'Yes,' he answered.

Isaac said, 'You see that I am old and may die soon. Take your bow and arrows, go out into the country, and kill an animal for me. Cook me some of that tasty food that I like, and bring it to me. After I have eaten it, I will give you my final blessing before I die.'

Thought: How do we react to the 'whims' of old people?

Prayer: Lord Jesus, please help us to be patient with the elderly people we know (especially . . .) remembering that they are nearing the end of their lives and need our gentle understanding. Amen.

Day 6

Genesis 27.5-10

While Isaac was talking to Esau, Rebecca was listening. So when Esau went out to hunt, she said to Jacob 'I have just heard your father say to Esau, "Bring me an animal and cook it for me. After I have eaten it, I will give you my blessing in the presence of the Lord before I die." Now, my son,' Rebecca continued, 'listen to me and do what I say. Go to the flock and pick out two fat young goats, so that I can cook them and make some of that food your father likes so much. You can take it to him to eat, and he will give you his blessing before he dies.'

Thought: Do we ever encourage or persuade someone to be deceitful and to do wrong?

Prayer: Father in Heaven, grant that we may never be guilty of persuading someone to do something which we know, in our hearts, is wrong. For Your Name's sake. Amen.

Day 7

Genesis 27.11-13

But Jacob said to his mother. 'You know that Esau is a hairy man, but I have smooth skin. Perhaps my father will touch me and find out that I am deceiving him; in this way I will bring a curse on myself instead of a blessing.'

His mother answered, 'Let any curse against you fall on me, my son; just do as I say, and go and get the goats for me.'

Thought: Jacob's only fear was that he would be found out!

Prayer: Dear Father God, help us to see clearly the difference between right and wrong, and to obey you through love, and not through fear of being found out. Amen.

Week 39

Day 1

Genesis 27.14-17

So he went to get them and brought them to her, and she cooked the kind of food that his father liked. Then she took Esau's best clothes, which she kept in the house, and put them on Jacob. She put the skins of the goats on his arms and on the hairless part of his neck. She handed him the tasty food, together with the bread she had baked.

Thought: Are there times when we seek to disguise our true selves?

Prayer: Lord, You know us as we really are, and love us just the same. Thank You for that knowledge. Amen.

Day 2

Genesis 27.18-20

Then Jacob went to his father and said, 'Father!'

'Yes,' he answered. 'Which of my sons are you?'

Jacob answered 'I am your elder son Esau; I have done as you told me. Please sit up and eat some of the meat that I have brought you, so that you can give me your blessing.'

Isaac said, 'How did you find it so quickly, my son?'

Jacob answered, 'The Lord your God helped me to find it.'

Thought: Which of Jacob's two lies do you think was the worst?

Prayer: Lord, please keep us from the habit of lying, because we know that one lie leads to another, and that lying is a habit it is very hard to break. Amen.

Day 3

Genesis 27.21-4

Isaac said to Jacob, 'Please come closer so that I can touch you. Are you really Esau?' Jacob moved closer to his father, who felt him and said, 'Your voice sounds like Jacob's voice, but your arms feel like Esau's arms.' He did not recognise Jacob, because his arms were hairy like Esau's. He was about to give him his blessing, but asked again, 'Are you really Esau?'

'I am,' he answered.

Thought: 'The path of deceit forbids retreat . . . ' True or false?

Prayer: Thank You, Lord Jesus, that we can always turn to You for forgiveness, which allows us to make a new start, even though we may have to live with the consequences of our wrong-doing. Amen.

Day 4

Genesis 27.25-7

Isaac said, 'Bring me some of the meat. After I have eaten it, I will give you my blessing.' Jacob brought it to him, and he also brought him some wine to drink. Then his father said to him, 'Come closer and kiss me, my son.' As he came up to kiss him, Isaac smelt his clothes - so he gave him his blessing. He said, 'The pleasant smell of my son is like the smell of a field which the Lord has blessed.'

Thought: Can you think of someone else who was betrayed by a kiss?

Prayer: Lord, thank You for kisses that are a sign of love and trust; may we give and receive them bearing this in mind. Amen.

Day 5

Genesis 27.28-9

'May God give you dew from heaven and make your fields fertile! May he give you plenty of corn and wine! May nations be your servants, and may peoples bow down before you. May you rule over all your relatives, and may your mother's descendants bow down before you. May those who curse you be cursed, and may those who bless you be blessed.'

Thought: Do you think that Isaac asked for the *best things* for his son? Think of someone close to you, and pray for God's blessing on them.

Prayer: Dear Father God, You know how much I care for . . . Please grant them the blessing of . . . and may they come to know You better, and serve You faithfully, all the days of their life. Amen.

Day 6

Genesis 27.30-2, 35

Isaac finished giving his blessing, and as soon as Jacob left, his brother Esau came in from hunting. He also cooked some tasty food and took it to his father. He said, 'Please, father, sit up and eat some of the meat that I have brought you, so that you can give me your blessing.'

'Who are you?' Isaac asked.

'Your elder son Esau,' he answered . . .

Isaac answered, 'Your brother came and deceived me. He has taken away your blessing.'

Thought: Wrongs cannot always be righted.

Prayer: Dear God, although You always forgive us our wrongdoing, we know that sometimes our actions create situations that cannot be reversed. Remind us of this before we act. Amen.

Day 7

Genesis 27.41-4

Esau hated Jacob, because his father had given Jacob the blessing. He thought, 'The time to mourn my father's death is near; then I will kill Jacob.'

But when Rebecca heard about Esau's plan, she sent for Jacob and said, 'Listen, your brother Esau is planning to get even with you and kill you. Now, my son, do what I say. Go at once to my brother Laban in Haran, and stay with him for a while, until your brother's anger cools down . . . '

Thought: Mothers can have a lot of influence and power.

Prayer: Lord Jesus, please give wisdom to those who are mothers; help them to use their influence for good, and fill them with so much love that it overflows to everyone in the family, for Your dear sake. Amen.

Week 40

For the next three weeks we are going to look at the Old Testament book of Nehemiah, which is a kind of diary written by a Jew, who, after being captured during the war with Babylon, was given the job of cup-bearer to the Emperor Artaxerxes. Nehemiah used his position to good advantage and was granted permission to set in hand the rebuilding of the holy city of Jerusalem.

Day 1

Nehemiah 1.1, 2, 3, 4

I, Nehemiah was in Susa, the capital city. Hanani, one of my brothers, arrived from Judah with a group of other men . . . they . . . told me that the walls of Jerusalem were still broken down and that the gates had not been restored since the time they were burnt. When I heard all this, I sat down and wept. For several days I mourned and did not eat. I prayed to God.

Thought: Does bad news bring us to our knees?

Prayer: Please God, give us a real love and concern for our fellow Christians in other places, so that we may pray earnestly for them and be used to help them. Amen.

Day 2

Nehemiah 2.1-3

One day four months later, when Emperor Artaxerxes was dining, I took the wine to him. He had never seen me look sad before, so he asked, 'Why are you looking so sad? You aren't ill, so it must be that you're unhappy.'

I was startled and answered, 'May Your Majesty live for ever! How can I help looking sad when the city where my ancestors are buried is in ruins and its gates have been destroyed by fire?'

Thought: A neglected church often reflects the neglected worship of God.

Prayer: Please God, help us to take our part in ensuring that the outward appearance of our church reflects the care and concern that is shown for the worship of You within it. Amen.

Day 3

Nehemiah 2.4-5

The emperor asked, 'What is it that you want?'

I prayed to the God of Heaven, and then I said to the emperor, 'If Your Majesty is pleased with me and is willing to grant my request, let me go to the land of Judah, to the city where my ancestors are buried, so that I can rebuild the city.'

Thought: Do we make quick prayers for guidance?

Prayer: Lord, teach us to turn to You instantly when we are asked questions that need precise answers. Amen.

Day 4

Nehemiah 2.7-8

Then I asked him to grant me the favour of giving me letters to the governors of West Euphrates Province, instructing them to let me travel to Judah. I asked also for a letter to Asaph, keeper of the royal forests, instructing him to supply me with timber for the gates of the fort that guards the Temple, for the city walls, and for the house I was to live in. The Emperor gave me all I asked for, because God was with me.'

Thought: We should not be afraid of asking for resources that will enable us to do God's work.

Prayer: Lord, make us bold in asking for material help for unselfish needs, in order to ensure that Your work goes forward. Amen.

Day 5

Nehemiah 2.11-14

I went on to Jerusalem, and for three days I did not tell anyone what God had inspired me to do for Jerusalem. Then in the middle of the night I got up and went out, taking a few of my companions with me. The only animal we took was the donkey that I rode on. It was still night as I left the city through the Valley Gate on the west and went south past Dragon's Fountain to the Rubbish Gate. As I went, I inspected the broken walls of the city and the gates that had been destroyed by fire. Then on the east side of the city I went north to the Fountain Gate and the King's Pool.

Thought: Plan before you act!

Prayer: Almighty God, remind us of the need to be quiet and alone with You, so that we can think and plan the best way to set about Your work, before we begin it. Amen.

Day 6

Nehemiah 2.16

None of the local officials knew where I had been or what I had been doing. So far I had not said anything to any of my fellow Jews - the priests, the leaders, the officials, or anyone else who would be taking part in the work.

Thought: Do not 'broadcast' your quiet times, prayers or retreats!

Prayer: Lord, our times alone with You are precious and secret. Help us to keep them that way. Amen.

Day 7

Nehemiah 2.17-18

But now I said to them, 'See what trouble we are in because Jerusalem is in ruins and its gates are destroyed! Let's rebuild the city walls and put an end to our disgrace.' And I told them how God had been with me and helped me, and what the emperor had said to me.

They responded, 'Let's start rebuilding!' And they got ready to start the work.

Thought: 'Let's start rebuilding!'

Prayer: God our Father, there is always rebuilding to be done in our relationships with our family, business or work associates, or with people within our Church. Sometimes we also need to rebuild our relationship with You. Help us to consider carefully what needs to be done and start today. Amen.

Week 41

Day 1

Nehemiah 2.19-20

When Sanballat, Tobiah, and an Arab named Geshem heard what we were planning to do, they laughed at us and said, 'What do you think you're doing? Are you going to rebel against the emperor?'

Thought: There will always be those who laugh and mock and misunderstand our motives.

Prayer: Almighty God, we know there will always be people who will ridicule our attempts to link our Christian faith with action, and who will misunderstand our motives. Help us to turn a deaf ear to their words, knowing we are doing Your will. Amen.

Day 2

Nehemiah 4.1-2

When Sanballat heard that we Jews had begun rebuilding the wall, he was furious and began to ridicule us. In front of his companions and the Samaritan troops he said, 'What do these miserable Jews think they're doing? Do they intend to rebuild the city? Do they think that by offering sacrifices they can finish the work in one day? Can they make building-stones out of heaps of burnt rubble?'

Thought: We should not despise the work of others.

Prayer: Lord God, please help us to refrain from criticising the work of others, while our own hands are idle. Amen.

Day 3

Nehemiah 4.3, 4, 6

Tobiah was standing there beside him, and he added, 'What kind of wall could they ever build? Even a fox could knock it down.'

I prayed, 'Listen to them mocking us, O God! Let their ridicule fall on their own heads . . . ' So we went on rebuilding the wall, and soon it was half its full height, because the people were eager to work.

Thought: A lot can be achieved when people are eager to work!

Prayer: Almighty God, whatever our Christian service may be, may we not give our time and energy grudgingly, but make us eager to work for the building of Your Kingdom. Amen.

Day 4

Nehemiah 4.7-9

Sanballat, Tobiah, and the people of Arabia, Ammon, and Ashdod heard that we were making progress in rebuilding the wall of Jerusalem and that the gaps in the wall were being closed, and they were very angry. So they all plotted together to come and attack Jerusalem and create confusion, but we prayed to our God and kept men on guard against them day and night.

Thought: 'Watch and pray.'

Prayer: Dear God, teach us to pray, and then to do all in our power to prevent the Enemy damaging Your work. Amen.

Day 5

Nehemiah 4.14

I saw that the people were worried, so I said to them and to their leaders and officials, 'Don't be afraid of our enemies. Remember how great and terrifying the Lord is, and fight for your fellow-countrymen, your children, your wives, and your homes.'

Thought: 'Don't be afraid . . . remember how great . . . the Lord is.'

Prayer: Lord, we pray today for all those who are afraid, particularly those who are afraid of losing their fellow countrymen, their wives, their children, and their homes because of war. We think particularly of those in . . . Please be with them; and show us how we may give them practical help. Amen.

Day 6

Nehemiah 4.15-17

Our enemies heard that we had found out what they were plotting, and they realised that God had defeated their plans. Then all of us went back to rebuilding the wall.

From then on half of my men worked and half stood guard, wearing coats of armour and armed with spears, shields, and bows. And our leaders gave their full support to the people.

Thought: A leader's job is to 'support the people.'

Prayer: We pray today for those who have the responsibility of leadership (particularly . . .). Please help them, Lord, to be an example and support to those they seek to lead. Amen.

Day 7

Nehemiah 4.19-20

I told the people and their officials and leaders, 'The work is spread out over such a distance that we are widely separated from one another on the wall. If you hear the bugle, gather round me. Our God will fight for us.'

Thought: 'Separated by distance . . . '

Prayer: Lord, we think today of those we love who are separated from us by distance, and who are engaged in building a different part of the Christian 'wall' (especially . . .). Help us to keep in touch by letters, telephone calls, visits, and by our prayers. Amen.

Week 42

Day 1

Nehemiah 5.1-4
Some time later many of the people, both men and women, began to complain against their fellow-Jews. Some said, 'We have large families, we need corn to keep us alive.'

Others said, 'We have had to mortgage our fields and vineyards and houses to get enough corn to keep us from starving.'

Still others said, 'We had to borrow money to pay the royal tax on our fields and vineyards.'

Thought: They never would hear
    But turn the deaf ear
    As a matter they had no concern in.
Jonathan Swift (1667-1745)

Prayer: God our Father, we pray today for those who are worried about how to pay for food, or mortgage repayments, or taxes. Show us how we may add practical help to our prayers. Amen.

Day 2

Nehemiah 5.6, 7, 8, 9, 12
When I heard their complaints I was angry . . . I called a public assembly to deal with the problem . . . The leaders were silent and could find nothing to say. Then I said, 'What you are doing is wrong! You ought to obey God and do what's right . . .'

The leaders replied, 'We'll do as you say. We'll give the property back and not try to collect the debts.'

Thought: Are you prepared to cancel all debts?

Prayer: Lord, You know we often set limits on our generosity to others. Teach us to give, rather than lend, expecting nothing back and trusting You to supply all our needs. Amen.

Day 3

Nehemiah 5.14-15
During all the twelve years that I was governor of the land of Judah, from the twentieth year that Artaxerxes was emperor until his thirty-second year, neither my relatives nor I ate the food I was entitled to have as governor.

Every governor who had been in office before me had been a burden to the people and had demanded forty silver coins a day for food and wine. Even their servants had oppressed the people. But I acted differently, because I honoured God.

Thought: 'I acted differently because I honoured God'

Prayer: Lord, because we are Your followers, give us the courage and determination to 'act differently' in everyday situations, putting other people's needs before our own. Amen.

Day 4

Nehemiah 6.15-16
After fifty-two days of work the entire wall was finished on the twenty-fifth day of the month of Elul. When our enemies in the surrounding nations heard this, they realised that they had lost face, since everyone knew that the work had been done with God's help.

Thought: 'The work had been done with God's help!'

Prayer: Our prayer today is a verse of a well-known hymn:
'Thy mercy will not fail us, Nor leave thy work undone,
With thy right hand to help us, The vict'ry shall be won;
And then, by men and angels, Thy name shall be adored,
And this shall be their anthem: one church, one faith, one Lord!'
E. H. Plumtre (1821-91)

Day 5

Nehemiah 8.1-3, 13
By the seventh month the people of Israel were all settled in their towns. On the first day of that month they all assembled in Jerusalem, in the square just inside the Water Gate. They asked Ezra, the priest and scholar of the Law which the Lord had given Israel through Moses, to get the book of the Law. So Ezra brought it to the place where the people had gathered - men, women, and the children who were old enough to understand. There in the square by the gate he read the Law to them from dawn until noon, and they all listened attentively.

Thought: Bible Studies are not a new idea!

Prayer: Almighty God, help us not only to read Your Word, but to study and understand it, so that we can put its teaching into practice. Amen.

Day 6

Nehemiah 10.28-9

We, the people of Israel, the priests, the Levites, the temple guards, the temple musicians, the temple workmen, and all others who in obedience to God's Law have separated themselves from the foreigners living in our land, we, together with our wives and all our children old enough to understand, do hereby join with our leaders in an oath . . . that we will live according to God's Law which God gave through his servant Moses; that we will obey all that the Lord, our Lord, commands us; and that we will keep all his laws and requirements.

Thought: Has your family or Church made a corporal commitment to obey God?

Prayer: Day by day, dear Lord
Of thee three things I pray,
To see thee more clearly,
To love thee more dearly,
To follow thee more nearly
Day by day.

Richard of Chichester (1197-1253)

Day 7

Nehemiah 12.27, 43

When the city wall of Jerusalem was dedicated, the Levites were brought in from wherever they were living, so that they could join in celebrating the dedication with songs of thanksgiving and with the music of cymbals and harps . . . That day many sacrifices were offered, and the people were full of joy because God had made them very happy. The women and the children joined in the celebration, and the noise they all made could be heard far and wide.

Thought: 'God had made them very happy.'

Prayer: Lord, we thank You for the happy times we have; for birthday celebrations, festivals, parties, and family gatherings, and for joyful Church services, where we celebrate different seasons in the Church year, or for the completion of some new work that has been done in Your Name. Be with us at these times, and increase our joy. Amen.

Week 43

*Jesus seldom preached long sermons, when He was here on earth;
instead he often told stories with a hidden meaning, or used
everyday circumstances to teach people about God.
This week we see Him 'in action'!*

Day 1

St Matthew 21.12-13

Jesus went into the Temple and drove out all those who were buying and selling there. He overturned the tables of the money-changers and the stools of those who sold pigeons, and said to them, 'It is written in the Scriptures that God said, "My Temple will be called a house of prayer." But you are making it a hideout for thieves!'

Thought: Is your Church 'a house of prayer'?

Prayer: Lord, sometimes our Church is so noisy that we forget it is meant to be a house of prayer; forgive us when we are guilty of treating it like a market-place. Amen.

Day 2

St Matthew 21.28-31

'Now, what do you think? There was once a man who had two sons. He went to the elder one and said, "Son, go and work in the vineyard today."

"I don't want to," he answered, but later he changed his mind and went. Then the father went to the other son and said the same thing.

"Yes, sir," he answered, but he did not go. Which one of the two did what the father wanted?'

'The elder one,' they answered.

So Jesus said to them, 'I tell you: the tax collectors and the prostitutes are going into the Kingdom of God ahead of you.'

Thought: Is it a good or bad thing to change your mind?

Prayer: Please, Lord Jesus, show us the right thing to do, and the right way to go, in all situations, and when we see Your will clearly, help us to do it, however inconvenient it may be. Amen.

Day 3

St Luke 14.15-17

When one of the men sitting at table heard this, he said to Jesus, 'How happy are those who will sit down at the feast in the Kingdom of God!'

Jesus said to him, 'There was once a man who was giving a great feast to which he invited many people. When it was time for the feast, he sent his servant to tell his guests, "Come, everything is ready!"'

Thought: Invitations can be accepted or rejected.

Prayer: Thank You, Lord, for Your invitation to be a guest at Your kingdom banquet. I accept with gratitude. Amen.

Day 4

St Luke 14.18-20

'But they all began, one after another, to make excuses. The first one told the servant, "I have bought a field and must go and look at it; please accept my apologies." Another one said, "I have bought five pairs of oxen and am on my way to try them out; please accept my apologies." Another one said, "I have just got married, and for that reason I cannot come."'

Thought: Do your possessions or family responsibilities take first place in your life?

Prayer: Dear Father God, we may not have fields and oxen, or be newly married, but we confess that our homes, families and hobbies, take up most of our time. Forgive us, and help us to put first things first. Amen.

Day 5

St Luke 14.21-2

'The servant went back and told all this to his master. The master was furious and said to his servant, "Hurry out to the streets and alleys of the town, and bring back the poor, the crippled, the blind, and the lame." Soon the servant said, "Your order has been carried out, sir, but there is room for more."'

Thought: Those who have least, often respond more readily to the Christian message than those who have much. Do you agree?

Prayer: Lord, it often seems that those who are poor, or lonely, or disabled, accept your message more readily than those who are healthy and wealthy and feel no need of You; give *us* a greater concern for our eternal future. Amen.

Day 6

St Luke 14.23-4

'So the master said to the servant, "Go out to the country roads and lanes and make people come in, so that my house will be full. I tell you all that none of those men who were invited will taste my dinner!"'

Thought: Opportunities may only come once!

Prayer: Heavenly Father, help us to ensure that the people we know, at least *hear* about You, and Your invitation to be a forgiven guest at Your heavenly banquet; whether they will accept it or not. Amen.

Day 7

St Matthew 22.15, 17-21

The Pharisees went off and made a plan to trap Jesus with questions . . 'Tell us, then, what do you think? Is it against our Law to pay taxes to the Roman Emperor, or not?'

Jesus, however, was aware of their evil plan, and so he said, 'You hyprocrites! Why are you trying to trap me? Show me the coin for paying the tax!'

They brought him the coin, and he asked them, 'Whose face and name are these?'

'The Emperor's,' they answered.

So Jesus said to them, 'Well, then, pay the Emperor what belongs to the Emperor, and pay God what belongs to God.'

Thought: Do you pay your legal taxes, but forget what you owe to God?

Prayer: Heavenly Father, we pay our earthly taxes, not because we *want* to, but because we *have* to; but help us to give back to You a fair share of our time and money, just because we love You. Amen.

Remember, there are special readings for Easter and Christmas, at the end of the book.

GRACES FOR SPECIAL OCCASIONS

'Then Jesus took the five loaves and the two fish, looked up to heaven and gave thanks to God.' (St. Mark 6.41)
'Then Jesus took a cup, gave thanks to God, and said . . . ' (Luke 22.17)

A prayer of thanks before food helps us to keep in touch with God at regular times throughout the day. Why not try to make this a regular habit, first choosing a suitable grace from those I have suggested and then putting your thanks into your own words?

A formal grace.
For what we are about to receive may the Lord make us truly thankful.
Amen.

At an informal meal with friends.
For food and friends and fellowship, we thank You, Lord.

At a meal for famine relief.
May we who have plenty remember those who have nothing, and may we waste nothing that is good to eat and comes from Your hand, O God. Amen.

At breakfast.
(1) We thank you, Lord, for this good food. Be with us as we eat it, and stay with each one of us throughout the coming day. In Your name we ask it. Amen.

(2) For sleep to refresh us, for a family to love us, and for food to satisfy our hunger, we thank You Lord. Amen.

The simplest grace.
Thank you, Lord Jesus, for this nice breakfast/Dinner/tea. Amen.

* *A family reunion.*
Thank You, God, for bringing us together again, as members of a family. Be with us as we talk and eat together and fill our hearts with joy and gratitude. Amen.

A singing grace.
> All good gifts around us
> Are sent from heaven above.
> Then thank the Lord, O thank the Lord,
> For all His love. Amen.

A grace in rhyme.
> Heavenly Father, kind and good
> Who does give your children food:
> Accept the thanks we gladly bring,
> Thanks to God for everything. Amen.

A picnic grace.
We thank You, Father, for the novelty and fun of eating meals out of doors and for this food which we are about to enjoy. Amen.

A party.
Dear Lord Jesus, Thank You for this happy day, Please bless . . . on their birthday, and all of us who are joining in the fun of their party and sharing this lovely food. Amen.

An adult dinner party.
For the pleasure of good food, pleasant company and stimulating conversation may God give us thankful hearts. Amen.

A working lunch.
Lord, As we meet together and share this simple food may we be granted wisdom to also share thoughts and ideas that come from You and enable us to enrich our fellowship and extend our work. Amen.

Christmas.
We thank You, Lord, for all the joys of Christmas and for this special meal with which we celebrate Your birth. Amen.

Before a journey.
We thank you, Lord, for this food and ask for a safe journey for those who travel today. Bless them and keep them from harm we pray You. Amen.

A birthday.
As we thank you for this food, Lord, we thank You, too for the one whose birth we celebrate today. Please bless them and keep them safe throughout the coming year. Amen.

GRACES FOR EVERYDAY USE

We ask you, Lord, to provide for the needs of others and give us thankful hearts. Amen.

For healthy appetites and the means to satisfy them, we thank You, Lord. Amen.

Lord, give us grateful and thankful hearts for this food that is set before us now. Amen.

Lord, we ask You to bless this food, and show us how we can help to supply the needs of those in want. For Your sake. Amen.

For health and food and all Your gifts, Lord we thank You. Amen.

We thank You, Lord, for this food, and ask You to bless all those who have worked in so many ways so that we might be fed. Amen.

God bless this meal, God guide our ways, God give us grace our Lord to please. Amen.

For supplying our needs on this and every day we give You thanks Lord. Amen.

We thank You, Lord, for this food, and for the hands that have prepared it. Amen.

We give You thanks, Father, for providing this food to meet our daily needs. Amen.

For health and strength and daily food, we praise Your Name O Lord. Amen.

We thank You once again, dear Lord, for supplying our daily food. Amen.

May we never take Your provision for granted. Amen.

EASTER READINGS

You should begin these readings on the first day of Lent
For the next six weeks we are going to look at the events which led up
to the cruel death of Jesus on the Cross. This week we read about the
Passover supper, a special meal held each year to remind the Jewish
people how God had rescued them from slavery in Egypt.

Week 1

Day 1

St Luke 22.1-2
The time was near for the Festival of Unleavened Bread, which is called
the Passover. The chief priests and the teachers of the Law were afraid of
the people, and so they were trying to find a way of putting Jesus to death
secretly.

Thought: 'Fear is the parent of cruelty.'
                                        James Froude (1818-1894)

Prayer: Lord, You know we sometimes do wrong because we are afraid
(afraid of authority, of losing something, or someone, we value, or afraid of
being found out). Please forgive us and give us strength to be honest,
truthful, and straightforward in all our dealings. Amen.

Day 2

St Luke 22.3-6
Then Satan entered Judas, called Iscariot, who was one of the twelve
disciples. So Judas went off and spoke with the chief priests and the officers
of the temple guard about how he could betray Jesus to them. They were
pleased and offered to pay him money. Judas agreed to it and started looking
for a good chance to hand Jesus over to them without the people knowing
about it.

Thought: 'The love of money is the root of all evil.' Do you agree?

Prayer: Dear Father God, when we are tempted to obtain money by
doubtful means may Your Holy Spirit warn us to have nothing to do with
it. Amen.

Day 3

St Luke 22.8-12

Jesus sent off Peter and John with these instructions: 'Go and get the Passover meal ready for us to eat.'

'Where do you want us to get it ready?' they asked him.

He answered, 'As you go into the city, a man carrying a jar of water will meet you. Follow him into the house that he enters, and say to the owner of the house: "The Teacher says to you, Where is the room where my disciples and I will eat the Passover meal?" He will show you a large furnished room upstairs, where you will get everything ready.'

Thought: Ready obedience is a rare gift to find.

Prayer: Lord, give us ready ears, willing feet, and obedient hearts, so that You can tell us what to do and be sure that we will do it. Amen.

Day 4

St Luke 22.13-16

They went off and found everything just as Jesus had told them, and they prepared the Passover meal.

When the hour came, Jesus took his place at the table with the apostles. He said to them, 'I have wanted so much to eat this Passover meal with you before I suffer! For I tell you, I will never eat it until it is given its full meaning in the Kingdom of God.'

Thought: Is Jesus 'the host' at your meal-table?

Prayer: Lord Jesus, when we sit down to meals, please be with us as we eat and talk, and may our manners and conversation be such as You approve. Amen.

Day 5

St Luke 22.17-18

Then Jesus took a cup, gave thanks to God, and said, 'Take this and share it among yourselves. I tell you that from now on I will not drink this wine until the Kingdom of God comes.'

Thought: Sharing increases joy - it does not diminish it.

Prayer: Loving Lord Jesus, as You shared the wine at supper with Your friends help us to share Your love and forgiveness with others. Amen.

Day 6

St Luke 22.19-20

Then he took a piece of bread, gave thanks to God, broke it, and gave it to them, saying, 'This is my body, which is given for you. Do this in memory of me.' In the same way, he gave them the cup after the supper, saying, 'This cup is God's new covenant sealed with my blood, which is poured out for you.'

Thought: How often do we take bread and wine 'in memory' of Jesus?

Prayer: Lord, help us to be more faithful in gathering together with our fellow Christians and taking bread and wine in memory of You. Amen.

Day 7

St Luke 22.21-3

'But look! The one who betrays me is here at the table with me! The Son of Man will die as God has decided, but how terrible for that man who betrays him!'

Then they began to ask among themselves which one of them it could be who was going to do this.

Thought: Our own 'betrayal' of Jesus should concern us more than other peoples.

Prayer: Lord, we are so quick to look for faults in other people, and so slow to look critically at our own lives. Forgive us and make us aware when and where we fail You. Amen.

Week 2

After Jesus' last meal with his friends, which was somewhat spoiled by their arguments and boasting, Jesus went out and found a quiet place to pray, and it was there that Judas led the soldiers to arrest Him.

Day 1

St Luke 22.24-6

An argument broke out among the disciples as to which one of them should be thought of as the greatest. Jesus said to them, 'The kings of the pagans have power over their people, and the rulers are called "Friends of the People." But this is not the way it is with you; rather, the greatest one among you must be like the youngest, and the leader must be like the servant.'

Thought: Beware of wanting to be 'the greatest'!

Prayer: Lord Jesus, help us to find true joy in doing things for other people, knowing that by serving them we are serving You. Amen.

Day 2

St Luke 22.31-2

'Simon, Simon! Listen! Satan has received permission to test all of you, to separate the good from the bad, as a farmer separates the wheat from the chaff. But I have prayed for you, Simon, that your faith will not fail. And when you turn back to me, you must strengthen your brothers.'

Thought: Our own failures may sometimes be used to prevent others from making the same mistake.

Prayer: Lord, show us how we can use our failures to save other people from making the same mistakes, and help us to remember that prayer is a mighty weapon in times of temptation. Amen.

Day 3

St Luke 22.33-4

Peter answered, 'Lord, I am ready to go to prison with you and to die with you!'

'I tell you, Peter,' Jesus said, 'the cock will not crow tonight until you have said three times that you do not know me.'

Thought: 'Whoever thinks he is standing firm had better be careful that he does not fall.'   (1 Corinthians 10.12)

Prayer: Heavenly Father, we have no strength or power of our own to fight against the temptations which come upon us every day, so please give us the strength and power of Your Holy Spirit to help us. Amen.

Day 4

St Luke 22.39-42

Jesus left the city and went, as he usually did, to the Mount of Olives; and the disciples went with him. When he arrived at the place, he said to them, 'Pray that you will not fall into temptation.'

Then he went off from them about the distance of a stone's throw and knelt down and prayed. 'Father,' he said, 'if you will, take this cup of suffering away from me. Not my will, however, but your will be done.'

Thought: There are times when *we* have to pray, 'not my will . . . but your will be done . . . '

Prayer: Lord, we cannot always choose the path we would like to follow. Give us the courage to pray 'Your will be done' when the way is hard. Amen.

Day 5

St Luke 22.45-6

Rising from his prayer, he went back to the disciples and found them asleep, worn out by their grief. He said to them, 'Why are you sleeping? Get up and pray that you will not fall into temptation.'

Thought: It is often when we feel most worn out that we need to pray!

Prayer: Lord Jesus, we confess we sometimes get so worn out by the everyday business of living, that we find it hard to find time to meet with you. Please help us to get our priorities right. Amen.

Day 6

St Luke 22.47-8

Jesus was still speaking when a crowd arrived, led by Judas, one of the twelve disciples. He came up to Jesus to kiss him. But Jesus said, 'Judas, is it with a kiss that you betray the Son of Man?'

Thought: Kisses are a precious sign of love and friendship. Do not cheapen them!

Prayer: Thank you, Lord, for giving us the ability both to give and to receive love. Help us to value and appreciate the outward signs of affection that reflect true love within. Amen.

Day 7

St Luke 22.49-51

When the disciples who were with Jesus saw what was going to happen, they asked, 'Shall we use our swords, Lord?' And one of them struck the High Priest's slave and cut off his right ear.

But Jesus said, 'Enough of this!' He touched the man's ear and healed him.

Thought: Wrong cannot be put right by violence.

Prayer: Lord Jesus, help us to check the harsh word and the angry blow and to obey Your commands to return good for evil. Amen.

Week 3

Peter fails to keep his promise of loyalty and Jesus is tried before the Council and the State Governor, Pontius Pilate, a man who would like to have freed Jesus, if he had had the courage to do what he knew was right.

Day 1

St Luke 22.54-7

They arrested Jesus and took him away into the house of the High Priest; and Peter followed at a distance. A fire had been lit in the centre of the courtyard, and Peter joined those who were sitting round it. When one of the servant-girls saw him sitting there at the fire, she looked straight at him and said, 'This man too was with Jesus!'

But Peter denied it, 'Woman, I don't even know him!'

Thought: It is not always easy publicly to acknowledge Jesus as your friend.

Prayer: Lord Jesus, we do love You and try to follow You, and we think of You as our friend; help us to have the courage to acknowledge this with pride, when we are challenged in public. Amen.

Day 2

St Luke 22.58-60

After a little while a man noticed Peter and said, 'You are one of them, too!'

But Peter answered, 'Man, I am not!'

And about an hour later another man insisted strongly, 'There isn't any doubt that this man was with Jesus, because he also is a Galilean!'

But Peter answered, 'Man, I don't know what you are talking about!'

Thought: We should be identifiable as Christians by our behaviour, not by our nationality!

Prayer: Lord, we know that it should be a privilege to be called a Christian! Forgive us, and others, who do not match name and behaviour. Amen.

Day 3

St Luke 22.60, 61-2

At once, while he was still speaking, a cock crowed. The Lord turned round and looked straight at Peter, and Peter remembered that the Lord had said to him, 'Before the cock crows tonight, you will say three times that you do not know me.' Peter went out and wept bitterly.

Thought: Tears often come too late.

Prayer: O God, save us from the tears that come too late to wash away the consequences of our lack of faith, or love, or loyalty. Amen.

Day 4

St Luke 22.66-9

When day came, the elders, the chief priests, and the teachers of the Law met together, and Jesus was brought before the Council. 'Tell us,] they said, 'are you the Messiah?'

He answered, 'If I tell you, you will not believe me; and if I ask you a question, you will not answer. But from now on the Son of Man will be seated on the right of Almighty God.'

Thought: 'If I tell you, you will not believe . . . '

Prayer: Almighty God, Who came to live as man in an earthly home, so that we might believe and understand Your words; increase our faith and forgive our unbelief. Amen.

Day 5

St Luke 22.70-1

They all said, 'Are you, then, the Son of God?'

He answered them, 'You say that I am.'

And they said, 'We don't need any witnesses! We ourselves have heard what he said!'

Thought: To hear is not always to believe.

Prayer: Lord, we have many times heard the truth about You, but have failed to allow what we have heard to change the way we think and behave. Help us to both hear and obey. Amen.

Day 6

St Luke 23.1, 2, 13-14

The whole group rose up and took Jesus before Pilate, where they began to accuse him . . . Pilate called together the chief priests, the leaders, and the people, and said to them. 'You brought this man to me and said that he was misleading the people. Now, I have examined him here in your presence, and I have not found him guilty of any of the crimes you accuse him of.'

Thought: Do *we* make sound judgements?

Prayer: Lord, help us not to base our judgement of a situation upon gossip or prejudice but upon prayer-guided firsthand experience. Amen.

Day 7

St Luke 23.18-21

The whole crowd cried out, 'Kill him! Set Barabbas free for us!' (Barabbas had been put in prison for a riot that had taken place in the city, and for murder.)

Pilate wanted to set Jesus free, so he appealed to the crowd again. But they shouted back, 'Crucify him! Crucify him!'

Thought: That we, with Thee, may walk uncowed.
By fear of favour of the crowd.

Rudyard Kipling (1865-1936)

Prayer: Heavenly Father, You understand how much easier it is to 'follow the crowd' rather than stand alone for the things in which we believe. May Your Spirit give us the strength to stand firmly when we need to do so. Amen.

Week 4

Jesus dies and is buried by Joseph of Arimathea - a caring friend.

Day 1

St Luke 23.24-5

So Pilate passed the sentence on Jesus that they were asking for. He set free the man they wanted, the one who had been put in prison for riot and murder, and he handed Jesus over for them to do as they wished.

Thought: Who do you think was most to blame for the death of Jesus, the Chief Priests, Pontius Pilate, or the people in the crowd?

Prayer: Lord, sinful people were responsible for your death and we know that we too are sinful people. Forgive us and cleanse us from the sin which continues to hurt and grieve You. Amen.

Day 2

St Luke 23.32-4

Two other men, both of them criminals, were also led out to be put to death with Jesus. When they came to the place called "The Skull," they crucified Jesus there, and the two criminals, one on his right, and the other on his left. Jesus said, 'Forgive them, Father! They don't know what they are doing.'

Thought: 'It is better that ten guilty persons escape than one innocent suffer.'

Sir William Blackstone (1723-1780)

Do you agree?

Prayer: Almighty God, we pray today for men and women who, through injustice, are being ill-treated, imprisoned, or condemned to death for crimes of which they are innocent (especially . . .). Be with them in their loneliness, fear and frustration, and give them courage, strength and peace, and the knowledge that they are not forgotten. Amen.

Day 3

St Luke 23.39-43

One of the criminals hanging there hurled insults at him: 'Aren't you the Messiah? Save yourself and us!'

The other one, however, rebuked him, saying, 'Don't you fear God? You received the same sentence he did. Ours, however, is only right, because we are getting what we deserve for what we did; but he has done no wrong.' And he said to Jesus, 'Remember me, Jesus, when you come as King!'

Jesus said to him, 'I promise you that today you will be in Paradise with me.'

Thought: Do we *blame* the Lord Jesus, or *claim* his forgiveness?

Prayer: Lord Jesus Christ, forgive us when we blame You for troubles and difficulties that we have so often brought upon ourselves; and please use these situations to bring us nearer to You. Amen.

Day 4

St Luke 23.44-6
It was about twelve o'clock when the sun stopped shining and darkness covered the whole country until three o'clock; and the curtain hanging in the Temple was torn in two. Jesus cried out in a loud voice, 'Father! in your hands I place my spirit!' He said this and died.'

Thought: The death of Jesus glorified God - do our lives do the same?

Prayer: O Lord, Who by Your death opened up for us the way to heaven; help us, by our lives, to show others the way to You. Amen.

Day 5

St Luke 23.47-8
The army officer saw what had happened, and he praised God, saying, 'Certainly he was a good man!'

When the people who had gathered there to watch the spectacle saw what happened, they all went back home, beating their breasts in sorrow.

Thought: Do you think that the people who 'beat their breasts' were also part of the crowd that had so recently cried 'Kill him!'?

Prayer: Lord, we pray today for those who so easily fall in with the ugly mood and cruel behaviour of a crowd. Please save us from doing the same. Amen.

Day 6

St Luke 23.50-1
There was a man named Joseph from Arimathea, a town in Judaea. He was a good and honourable man who was waiting for the coming of the Kingdom of God. Although he was a member of the Council, he had not agreed with their decision and action.

Thought: 'He had not agreed with their decision and action.'

Prayer: Almighty God, we pray today for those Members of Parliament, councils, and committees, responsible for making far-reaching decisions (especially . . .). Give them wisdom to know whether to vote for, or against, the motions that will be raised. Amen.

Day 7

St Luke 23.52-4
He went into the presence of Pilate and asked for the body of Jesus. Then he took the body down, wrapped it in a linen sheet, and placed it in a tomb which had been dug out of solid rock and which had never been used. It was Friday, and the Sabbath was about to begin.

Thought: Sympathy is often best shown by practical help.

Prayer: Lord, when there is bereavement in a family, please show us the best way to help; not just with words but by taking on some of the ordinary, everyday matters that have to be attended to. Amen.

Week 5

The friends of Jesus find their sorrow is turned into very great joy!

Day 1

St Luke 23.55-7
The women who had followed Jesus from Galilee went with Joseph and saw the tomb and how Jesus' body was placed in it. Then they went back home and prepared the spices and perfumes for the body.

On the Sabbath they rested, as the Law commanded.

Thought: 'They prepared . . . they rested . . . '

Prayer: Dear Father God, You gave us one day a week to rest our bodies and minds and renew our spirits, and yet we are often so intent on *doing things* that we do not use Sunday in the way You intended. Help us to plan ahead so that we can use Your day rightly. Amen.

Day 2

St Luke 24.1-3
Very early on Sunday morning the women went to the tomb carrying the spices they had prepared. They found the stone rolled away from the entrance to the tomb, so they went in; but they did not find the body of the Lord Jesus.

Thought: Be prepared for the unexpected!

Prayer: Lord Jesus, life is full of surprises and we never know what a day will bring. Thank You for the unexpected joys - the kind word, the unplanned meeting, the thoughtful gift, and the good news which may come by telephone or letter, or the solving of a problem or difficulty which has been worrying us. Help us, too, to plan unexpected pleasures for others. Amen.

Day 3

St Luke 24.4-7
They stood there puzzled about this, when suddenly two men in bright shining clothes stood by them. Full of fear, the women bowed down to the ground, as the men said to them, 'Why are you looking among the dead for one who is alive? He is not here; he has been raised. Remember what he said to you while he was in Galilee: "The Son of Man must be handed over to sinful men, be crucified, and three days later rise to life." '

Thought: Find the EIGHT WORDS OF HOPE in today's reading and underline them!

Prayer: Lord, we thank You for the times when, in bereavement, we are sure that our loved ones are not here, but with You. Give this firm hope to all at this time who are grieving for someone they love (especially . . .). Amen.

Day 4

St Luke 24.8-9, 11-12

Then the women remembered his words, returned from the tomb, and told all these things to the eleven disciples and all the rest . . .

But the apostles thought that what the women said was nonsense, and they did not believe them. But Peter got up and ran to the tomb; he bent down and saw the linen wrappings but nothing else. Then he went back home amazed at what had happened.

Thought: The Christian message - 'sense' or 'nonsense'?

Prayer: Lord Jesus, we pray today for those who see the Christian message as 'nonsense' (especially . . .). We know that our words will not convince them, but we pray that, in time, Your Holy Spirit will touch their hearts and minds and they will accept You as their Lord and Saviour. Amen.

Day 5

St Luke 24.13-16

On that same day two of Jesus' followers were going to a village named Emmaus, about eleven kilometres from Jerusalem, and they were talking to each other about all the things that had happened. As they talked and discussed, Jesus himself drew near and walked along with them; they saw him, but somehow did not recognise him.

Thought: Are we happy for Jesus to 'listen in' to all our conversations?

Prayer: Dear Lord, we confess that there are many times when we would prefer You not to listen to our conversations: when we are quarrelling, speaking rudely, or talking about other people. Forgive us, and help us to be aware of Your presence and be happy for Your company. Amen.

Day 6

St Luke 24.17, 19, 20-1

Jesus said to them, 'What are you talking about to each other, as you walk along?' . . . 'The things that happened to Jesus of Nazareth,' they answered . . . 'Our chief priests and rulers handed him over to be sentenced to death, and he was crucified. And we had hoped that he would be the one who was going to set Israel free! Besides all that, this is now the third day since it happened.'

Thought: Do we doubt God's power when things do not turn out as expected?

Prayer: Almighty God, Lord of all power and might, forgive us when, with our little minds, we are unable to understand Your great plans for the redemption of the world by our Lord Jesus Christ, and, in our ignorance question Your wisdom and providence. Amen.

Day 7

St Luke 24.25-7
Then Jesus said to them, 'How foolish you are, how slow you are to believe everything the prophets said! Was it not necessary for the Messiah to suffer these things and then to enter his glory?' And Jesus explained to them what was said about himself in all the Scriptures, beginning with the books of Moses and the writings of all the prophets.

Thought: 'We present you with this Book, the most valuable thing that this world affords. Here is wisdom; this is the royal law; these are the lively oracles of God.'
            The presenting of a Bible at the Coronation service.

Prayer: Help us to value Your written Word, O God. To read it, to understand it, and to obey it. Amen.

Week 6

Jesus continues to meet and teach His followers before His final Ascension.

Day 1

St Luke 24.28-31

As they came near the village to which they were going, Jesus acted as if he were going farther; but they held him back, saying, 'Stay with us; the day is almost over and it is getting dark.' So he went in to stay with them. He sat down to eat with them, took the bread, and said the blessing; then he broke the bread and gave it to them. Then their eyes were opened and they recognised him, but he disappeared from their sight.

Thought: We may often recognise other Christians by their speech and behaviour.

Prayer: We thank You, Lord, for the times we recognise other Christians by their speech and behaviour, and for the oneness we feel at the special service of 'breaking of bread'. Amen.

Day 2

St Luke 24.32-5

They said to each other, 'Wasn't it like a fire burning in us when he talked to us on the road and explained the Scriptures to us?'

They got up at once and went back to Jerusalem, where they found the eleven disciples gathered together with the others and saying, 'The Lord is risen indeed! He has appeared to Simon!'

The two explained to them what had happened on the road, and how they had recognised the Lord when he broke the bread.

Thought: Do you share your Christian experiences?

Prayer: Lord Jesus, You speak to us in many different ways and in many different circumstances. Teach us to expect you to reveal yourself in our everyday lives and help us to share some of our experiences with our fellow Christians, so that we are all encouraged and strengthened. Amen.

Day 3

St Luke 24.36-9

'While the two were telling them this, suddenly the Lord himself stood among them and said to them, 'Peace be with you.'

They were terrified, thinking that they were seeing a ghost. But he said to them, 'Why are you alarmed? Why are these doubts coming up in your minds? Look at my hands and feet, and see that it is I myself. Feel me, and you will know, for a ghost doesn't have flesh and bones, as you can see I have.'

Thought: The presence of Jesus can be known without physical sight.

Prayer: Lord, sometimes we long to see and hear and touch you using our physical senses. Help us to remember your words: 'How happy are those who believe without seeing me.'* Amen.
[*John 20.29]

Day 4

St Luke 24.40-4
He said this and showed them his hands and his feet. They still could not believe, they were so full of joy and wonder; so he asked them, 'Have you anything here to eat?' They gave him a piece of cooked fish, which he took and ate in their presence.

Then he said to them, 'These are the very things I told you about while I was still with you: everything written about me in the Law of Moses, the writings of the prophets, and the Psalms had to come true.'

Thought: 'Full of joy and wonder!' Does that describe you?

Prayer: Lord Jesus, we know that Christians should be people who are full of joy and wonder, and yet we confess we are often miserable, and depressed and faithless. Help us to experience real joy, because of forgiven sin, real peace because there is nothing we cannot share with You, and real joy because of the beauty of the world You made; and give us a sense of wonder because we can so often see You at work in our lives, and the lives of others. Amen.

Day 5

St Luke 24.45-7
Then he opened their minds to understand the Scriptures, and said to them, 'This is what is written: the Messiah must suffer and must rise from death three days later, and in his name the message about repentance and the forgiveness of sins must be preached to all nations, beginning in Jerusalem.'

Thought: Resurrection, repentance, and forgiveness must be preached.

Prayer: Help us to hold fast to the threefold message of resurrection, repentance, and forgiveness, and give us the right words to pass it on to those we meet in our everyday lives, whenever we have the chance. Amen.

Day 6

St Luke 24.48-50

'You are witnesses of these things. And I myself will send upon you what my Father has promised. But you must wait in the city until the power from above comes down upon you.'

Then he led them out of the city as far as Bethany, where he raised his hands and blessed them.

Thought: Have *you* received the 'power from above'?

Prayer: Dear Lord Jesus, we are not capable of passing on Your message of forgiveness and love unless, every day, You continually re-fill us with the power of Your Holy Spirit. We ask you now to 'send us out in the power of your Spirit to live and work to Your praise and glory.'* Amen. [*A.S.B. Communion Prayer]

Day 7

St Luke 24.51-3

As he was blessing them, he departed from them and was taken up into heaven. They worshipped him and went back into Jerusalem, filled with great joy, and spent all their time in the Temple giving thanks to God.

Thought: All our time? Some of our time? None of our time?

Prayer: Lord, we have to confess that praising and thanking you does not come very high on our list of priorities. Help us to review the way we spend our time, so that You become a natural and important part of our daily lives. Amen.

CHRISTMAS READINGS

The readings for the next three weeks lead up to Christmas Day.
We start at the beginning of St Luke's gospel. Zechariah, the priest,
and Elizabeth, his wife, were relations of Mary the mother of Jesus.
This week we are going to read about the events preceding the birth of
John, Zechariah and Elizabeth's son, who, when he grew up, became a
prophet announcing the coming of the Lord Jesus to the people.

Week 1

Day 1

St Luke 1.5-7

During the time when Herod was king of Judaea, there was a priest
named Zechariah, who belonged to the priestly order of Abijah. His
wife's name was Elizabeth; she also belonged to a priestly family. They
both lived good lives in God's sight and obeyed fully all the Lord's laws
and commands. They had no children because Elizabeth could not have
any, and she and Zechariah were both very old.

Thought: 'They both lived good lives and obeyed fully all the Lord's laws.'

Prayer: Lord, thank you for Christian couples who live good lives and obey
all your laws (we think particularly of . . .). Please bless them and
continue to use them in your service. Amen.

Day 2

St Luke 1.8-10

One day Zechariah was doing his work as a priest in the Temple, taking
his turn in the daily service. According to the custom followed by the
priests, he was chosen by lot to burn incense on the altar. So he went into
the Temple of the Lord, while the crowd of people outside prayed during
the hour when the incense was burnt.

Thought: Do you pray while your Minister is taking the service?

Prayer: Almighty God, remind us to pray regularly for those taking our
Church services, so that we really become part of the worship (we think
especially of . . .). Amen.

Day 3

St Luke 1.11-13

An angel of the Lord appeared to him, standing on the right of the altar where the incense was burnt. When Zechariah saw him, he was alarmed and felt afraid. But the angel said to him, 'Don't be afraid, Zechariah! God has heard your prayer, and your wife Elizabeth will bear you a son. You are to name him John.'

Thought: 'Hast thou not seen, how thy heart's wishes have been, granted in what He ordaineth?'

J. Neander (1698)

Prayer: Heavenly Father, You know the most secret desires of our hearts. Please answer our prayers, if, in Your great wisdom, you know this would be for our good and within Your plan for our lives. Amen.

Day 4

St Luke 1.14-16

'How glad and happy you will be, and how happy many others will be when he is born! He will be a great man in the Lord's sight. He must not drink any wine or strong drink. From his very birth he will be filled with the Holy Spirit, and he will bring back many of the people of Israel to the Lord their God.'

Thought: 'The world's great men have not commonly been great scholars, nor its great scholars great men.'

Oliver Wendell Holmes, Snr. (1809-94)

Prayer: Lord, make us 'great' men, and women, and children, in the Lord's sight, and fill us with Your Holy Spirit so that we may have the joy of bringing people to You. Amen.

Day 5

St Luke 1.17

'He will go ahead of the Lord, strong and mighty like the prophet Elijah. He will bring fathers and children together again; he will turn disobedient people back to the way of thinking of the righteous; he will get the Lord's people ready for him.'

Thought: 'He will bring fathers and children together again . . . '

Prayer: Dear Father God, we pray today for all those who work to bring together husbands and wives, children and parents, and help them to make a new beginning. Be with them in their difficult work and give them continuing love and wisdom. We pray especially for . . . who are having problems at the moment. Amen.

Day 6

St Luke 1.18-19
Zechariah said to the angel, 'How shall I know if this is so? I am an old man, and my wife is old also.'

'I am Gabriel,' the angel answered. 'I stand in the presence of God, who sent me to speak to you and tell you this good news.'

Thought: We are never too young or too old for God to use!

Prayer: God of all power and might, we know You want to use all of us in Your service, whether we are children, young people, middle-aged, or old. Show us Your plan for our lives and direct us into Your paths. Amen.

Day 7

St Luke 1.23-5
When his period of service in the Temple was over, Zechariah went back home. Some time later his wife Elizabeth became pregnant, and did not leave the house for five months. 'Now at last the Lord has helped me,' she said.

Thought: Do we see a new baby as a gift from God?

Prayer: Loving Heavenly Father, thank You for the miracle of birth and the joy that a new baby brings (especially to . . .). Remind us to pray for the babies we know, that they may grow up to know You as their Lord and Saviour. Amen.

Week 2

During the next two weeks we are going to read St Luke's account of an angel's visit to a simple village girl, who was chosen by God to be the mother of Jesus, and of the exciting events that surrounded His birth.

Day 1

St Luke 1.26-8
In the sixth month of Elizabeth's pregnancy God sent the angel Gabriel to a town in Galilee named Nazareth. He had a message for a girl promised in marriage to a man named Joseph, who was a descendant of King David. The girl's name was Mary. The angel came to her and said, 'Peace be with you! The Lord is with you and has greatly blessed you!'

Thought: Messages from God do not always come via angels!

Prayer: Lord, give us hearing ears that will recognise Your voice whenever You speak to us, whether through the printed word, through other people, through circumstances, or through the unspoken word that directs us within our hearts and minds. Amen.

Day 2

St Luke 1.29-33
Mary was deeply troubled by the angel's message, and she wondered what the words meant. The angel said to her, 'Don't be afraid, Mary; God has been gracious to you. You will become pregnant and give birth to a son, and you will name him Jesus. He will be great and will be called the Son of the Most High God. The Lord God will make him a king, as his ancestor David was, and he will be the king of the descendants of Jacob for ever; his kingdom will never end!'

Thought: Do not be afraid.

Prayer: Dear Lord Jesus, You know we are sometimes afraid (of people, relationships, new situations, or medical treatment, of getting old, or of death). Please give us courage to go forward, strength to face the circumstances, and peace concerning the future. Amen.

Day 3

St Luke 1.34-8
Mary said to the angel, 'I am a virgin. How, then, can this be?'
   The angel answered, 'The Holy Spirit will come on you, and God's

power will rest upon you. For this reason the holy child will be called the Son of God. Remember your relative Elizabeth. It is said that she cannot have children, but she herself is now sixth months pregnant, even though she is very old. For there is nothing that God cannot do.'

'I am the Lord's servant,' said Mary; 'may it happen to me as you have said.' And the angel left her.

Thought: Miracles still happen!

Prayer: Lord, we often leave miracles out of our thinking, and limit You to working within natural means. Give us believing hearts which are capable of accepting and rejoicing over things that are outside our understanding. Amen.

Day 4

St Luke 1.39-45
Soon afterwards Mary got ready and hurried off to a town in the hill-country of Judaea. She went into Zechariah's house and greeted Elizabeth. When Elizabeth heard Mary's greeting, the baby moved within her. Elizabeth was filled with the Holy Spirit and said in a loud voice, 'You are the most blessed of all women, and blessed is the child you will bear! Why should this great thing happen to me, that my Lord's mother comes to visit me? For as soon as I heard your greeting, the baby within me jumped with gladness. How happy you are to believe that the Lord's message to you will come true!'

Thought: 'Sharing' with a close friend or relative can double joys and halve sorrows.

Prayer: Father, we thank You for the close friends and relations with whom we can share the joys and sorrows of our lives (especially . . .). Help us to be caring people, who really listen when people wish to share things with us. Amen.

Day 5

Mary's song of praise is called 'The Magnificant' and is sung in some churches each week as part of the service.

St Luke 1.46-50
Mary said,
   'My heart praises the Lord;
     my soul is glad because of God my Saviour,
   for he has remembered me, his lowly servant!

From now on all people will call me happy,
   because of the great things the Mighty God has done for me.
His name is holy;
   from one generation to another
   he shows mercy to those who honour him . . . '

Thought: Christians are meant to be glad and happy - not miserable and sad!

Prayer: Lord, we are glad because You have forgiven our sins and filled our lives with good thing (such as . . .). Thank You! Amen.

Day 6

St Luke 1.51-5
   'He has stretched out his mighty arm
      and scattered the proud with all their plans.
   He has brought down mighty kings
      from their thrones, and lifted up the lowly.
   He has filled the hungry with good things,
      and sent the rich away with empty hands.
   He has kept the promise he made to
      our ancestors, and has come to the help of his servant Israel.
   He has remembered to show mercy to Abraham,
      and to all his descendants for ever.'

Thought: Do we keep *our* promises.

Prayer: Lord, You are a God who keeps your promises. We grieve over our world at this time, because people have forgotten You and gone their own ways. Please scatter the proud with all their plans, bring down cruel and greedy rulers, and help those who are guided by Your Spirit to bring peace and order. Amen.

Day 7

St Luke 1.56-8
Mary stayed about three months with Elizabeth and then went back home. The time came for Elizabeth to have her baby, and she gave birth to a son. Her neighbours and relatives heard how wonderfully good the Lord had been to her, and they all rejoiced with her.

Thought: How often do we tell our neighbours and relatives how 'wonderfully good' the Lord has been to us?

Prayer: Lord, You have been wonderfully good to us in giving us the things we have. I am really grateful, Lord, and want to thank You. Amen.

Week 3

Day 1

St Luke 2.1-3
At that time the Emperor Augustus ordered a census to be taken throughout the Roman Empire. When this first census took place, Quirinius was the governor of Syria. Everyone, then, went to register himself, each to his own town.

Thought: Christians should set an example in obeying the law.

Prayer: Almighty God, we pray today for those in authority who make decisions about laws and regulations. Help us to set a good example by keeping the laws of our country and supporting those in authority. Amen.

Day 2

St Luke 2.4-7
Joseph went from the town of Nazareth in Galilee to the town of Bethlehem in Judaea, the birthplace of King David. Joseph went there because he was a descendant of David. He went to register with Mary, who was promised in marriage to him. She was pregnant, and while they were in Bethlehem, the time came for her to have her baby. She gave birth to her first son, wrapped him in strips of cloth and laid him in a manager - there was no room for them to stay in the inn.

Thought: Things do not always go according to plan!

Prayer: When we are called upon to deal with an emergecny, enable us to be calm and efficient as we cope with it, remembering that You are present with us in every situation. Amen.

Day 3

St Luke 2.8-12
There were some shepherds in that part of the country who were spending the night in the fields, taking care of their flocks. An angel of the Lord appeared to them, and the glory of the Lord shone over them. They were terribly afraid, but the angel said to them, 'Don't be afraid! I am here with good news for you, which will bring great joy to all the people. This very day in David's town your Saviour was born - Christ the Lord! And this is what will prove it to you: you will find a baby wrapped in strips of cloth and lying in a manager.'

Thought: God's messengers usually arrive unannounced!

Prayer: Heavenly Father, we never know when one of Your messengers will bring us a message from You that will motivate us to do something or go somewhere unexpectedly. When it happens, Lord, help us to obey You promptly. Amen.

Day 4

St Luke 2.13-14
Suddenly a great army of heaven's angels appeared with the angel, singing praises to God:

'Glory to God in the highest heaven, and peace on earth to those with whom he is pleased!'

Thought: Does your church singing sound like 'a great army of heaven's angels'? If not, how much does your voice contribute to the praise?

Prayer: Lord Jesus, when we are next in Church remind us that we are one of a great company of believers, scattered throughout the world to sing praises to You, and help us to join in the singing with enthusiasm and joy. Amen.

Day 5

If you have worked out the dates correctly this reading should come on Christmas Day - December 25th!

St Luke 2.15-17
When the angels went away from them back into heaven, the shepherds said to one another, 'Let's go to Bethlehem and see this thing that has happened, which the Lord has told us.'

So they hurried off and found Mary and Joseph and saw the baby lying in the manger. When the shepherds saw him, they told them what the angel had said about the child. All who heard it were amazed at what the shepherds said.

Thought: 'Let's go and see! So they hurried off and found . . . and saw. '

Prayer: Lord, this Christmas we celebrate Your birth by decorating our houses, eating a festive meal, giving each other presents, and entertaining our family and friends. Help us to make time to gather together with Your people and listen again to the story of Your coming to earth as a human baby, and to praise and worship You for Your goodness and mercy towards us and those we love. Amen.

Day 6

Boxing Day

St Luke 2.19-20

Mary remembered all these things and thought deeply about them. The shepherds went back, singing praises to God for all they had heard and seen; it had been just as the angel had told them.

Thought: Will we 'remember and think deeply' about the events of Christmas Day now that they are over?

Prayer: Lord, another Christmas Day has come and gone. Please help us to remember and think about You each day during this coming year, and not just at times of special celebration. Amen.

Day 7

St Matthew 2.1-2,11

Jesus was born in the town of Bethlehem in Judaea, during the time when Herod was king. Soon afterwards, some men who studied the stars came from the east to Jerusalem and asked, 'Where is the baby born to be the king of the Jews? We saw his star when it came up in the east, and we have come to worship him.'

They went into the house, and when they saw the child with his mother Mary, they knelt down and worshipped him. They brought out their gifts of gold, frankincense, and myrrh, and presented them to him.

Thought: What gifts can we bring to Jesus as we approach a New Year?

Prayer: Dear Lord Jesus, we offer You afresh the gift of ourselves, our home, our talents, our money, our time and our worship. Please use us and all we have to offer, in Your service. Amen.